Enjoy these Words of

Here's a Thougнт!

These words have improved

CONFIDENCE, SELF-ESTEEM, and WELL BEING

for THOUSANDS of people!

PASS IT ALONG · PASS IT ALONG
DETACHABLE THOUGHTS
PASS IT ALONG · PASS IT ALONG

Norm Caldwell

Enlightening

Words of Wisdom and Inspiratio

For use as BOOKMARKS,

or inside

GREETING CARDS, GIFTS, POCKETS

MY MOTHER'S PUBLISHING HOUSE

23933 Eureka Road
Taylor, MI 48180
Phone: (734) 287-2930
FAX: (734) 287-7788

ISBN 1-56273-178-5

Library of Congress Cataloging-in-Publication Data

PUBLISHED BY
My Mother's Publishing House

COVER AND GRAPHICS

Donna Stopera and Norm Caldwell

Why not write (or call), and let us know how much you enjoyed our book.

WE WILL DESIGN TAILOR-MADE WORDS OF WISDOM
FOR YOU OR YOUR ORGANIZATION.

Heres a Thought!™

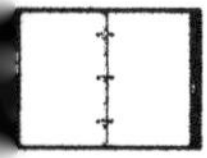

Norm Caldwell

How would you share yours?
In a briefcase, newspaper, mailbox,
include it in a card or letter,
in a book, in a box,
everyone has a daily planner, or just on
someone's desk ?

Detachable Thoughts

~ey make it easy to be THOUGHTFUL

YOU
'E IT AWAY
YET
'U KEEP IT!

TWO
BOOKS IN
ONE!

IMAGINE THAT! ■

TWO
BOOKS IN
ONE!

PASS IT ALONG
PASS IT ALONG
DETACHABLE
THOUGHTS'
PASS IT ALONG
PASS IT ALONG

YOU
GIVE IT AWAY
YET
YOU KEEP IT!

Reflections

HERE'S A THOUGHT!

MY MOTHER'S
PUBLISHING HOUSE

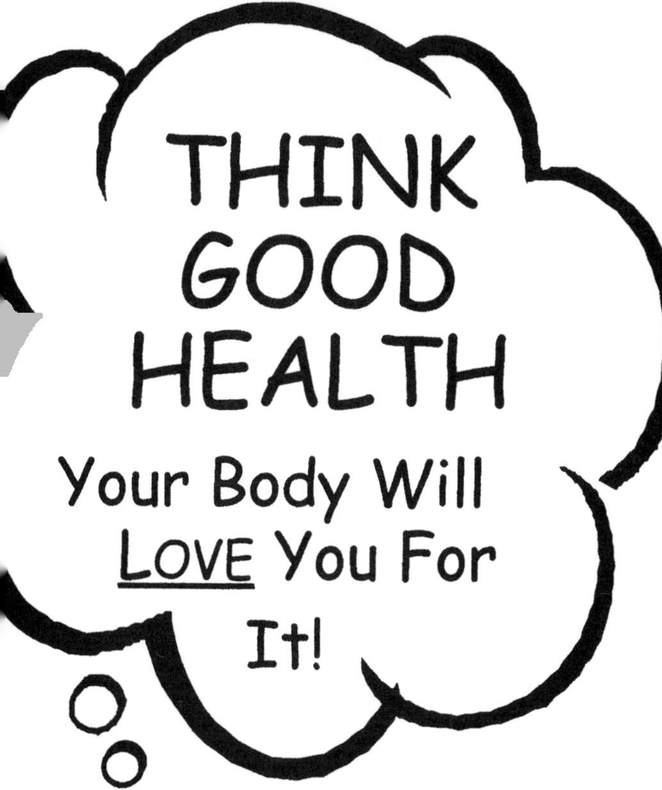
THINK
GOOD
HEALTH
Your Body Will
LOVE You For
It!

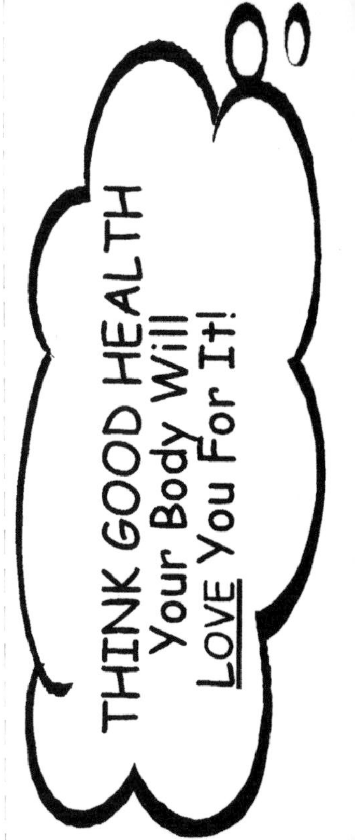
THINK GOOD HEALTH
Your Body Will
LOVE You For It!

Reflections

HERE'S A THOUGHT!

MY MOTHER'S
PUBLISHING HOUSE

THE TRUTH

CAN

Clear Your Mind
and
Cleanse your Soul!

THE TRUTH
Can Clear Your Mind and
Cleanse your Soul!

Reflections

HERE'S A THOUGHT!

MY MOTHER'S
PUBLISHING HOUSE

SEE THE

WHOLE

PICTURE

Expand Your View!

See the

WHOLE PICTURE

Expand Your View!

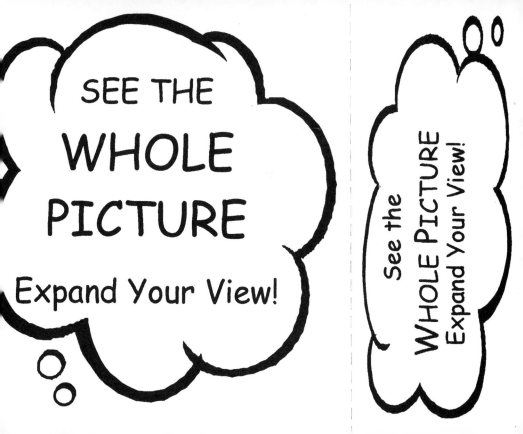

Reflections

HERE'S A THOUGHT!

MY MOTHER'S
PUBLISHING HOUSE

Belief
In God
DEVELOPS
Belief
In Self!

BELIEF IN GOD
DEVELOPS
Belief in Self!

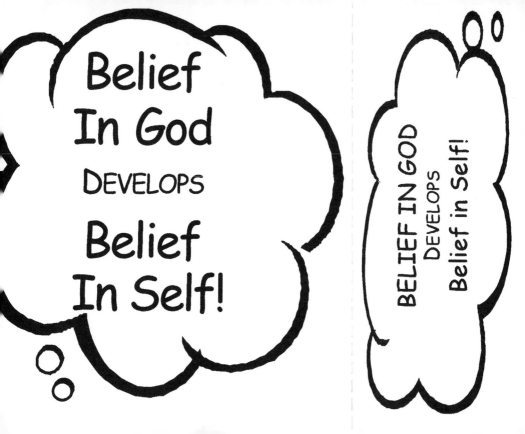

Reflections

HERE'S A THOUGHT!

> MY MOTHER'S
> PUBLISHING HOUSE

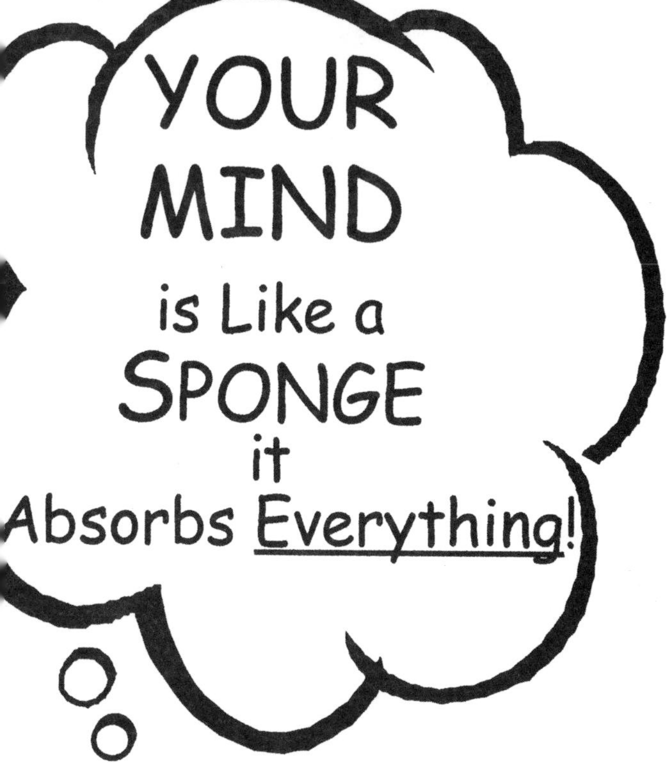
YOUR
MIND
is Like a
SPONGE
it
Absorbs Everything!

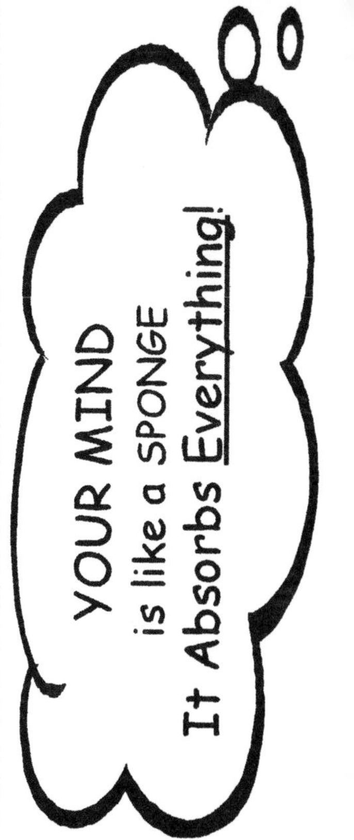
YOUR MIND
is like a SPONGE
It Absorbs Everything!

Reflections

HERE'S A THOUGHT!

MY MOTHER'S PUBLISHING HOUSE

SHARE

New Idea's

THEY LOVE

Making FRIENDS!

SHARE NEW IDEA'S

THEY LOVE Making FRIENDS!

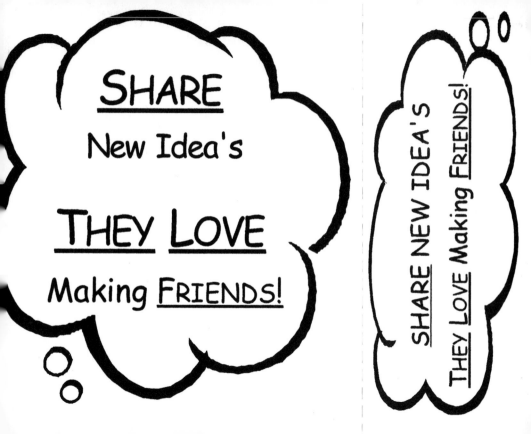

Reflections

HERE'S A THOUGHT!

> MY MOTHER'S
> PUBLISHING HOUSE

How Fast

Can Your Mind Learn

That's Right

This Fast!

HOW FAST
Can Your Mind Learn?
That's Right
THIS FAST!

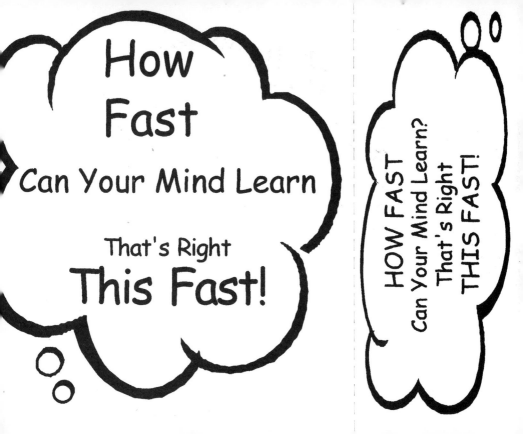

Reflections

HERE'S A THOUGHT!

MY MOTHER'S
PUBLISHING HOUSE

LET YOUR
WISDOM
and
Courage
STEP FORWARD
Then Stay in Step!

LET YOUR
WISDOM AND COURAGE
STEP FORWARD
Then Stay In Step!

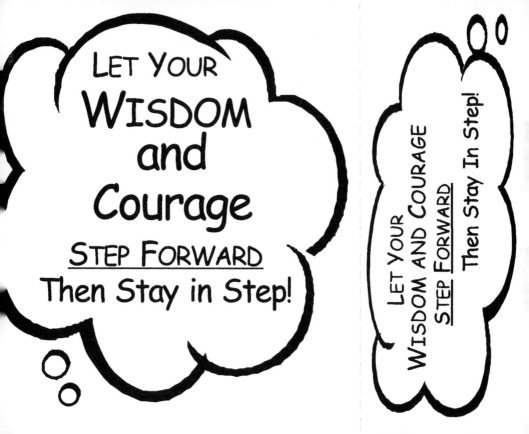

Reflections

HERE'S A THOUGHT!

MY MOTHER'S
PUBLISHING HOUSE

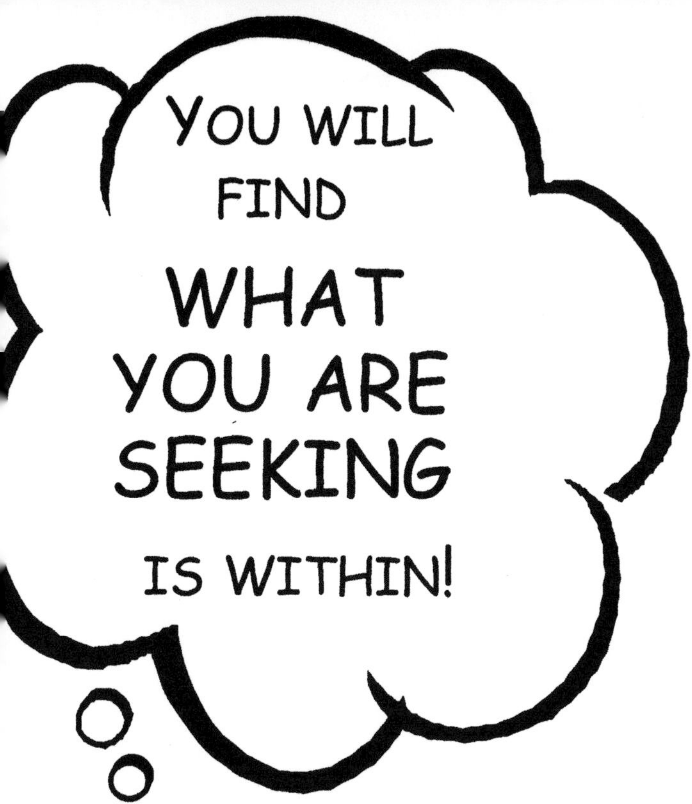
YOU WILL
FIND
WHAT
YOU ARE
SEEKING
IS WITHIN!

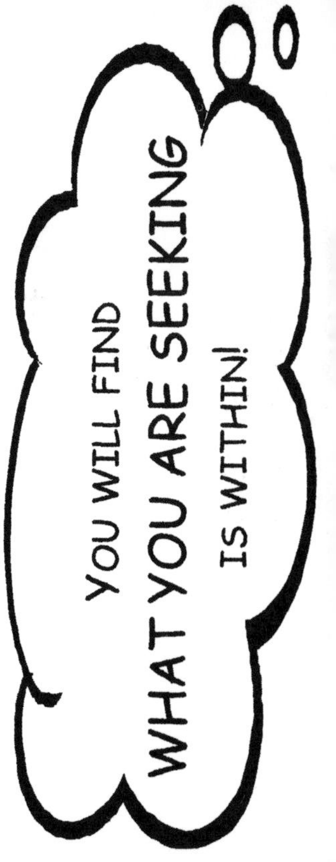
YOU WILL FIND
WHAT YOU ARE SEEKING
IS WITHIN!

Reflections

HERE'S A THOUGHT!

MY MOTHER'S
PUBLISHING HOUSE

Being Yourself Is <u>Easier</u> than Being What's Expected!

BEING YOURSELF
Is Easier than
Being What's Expected!

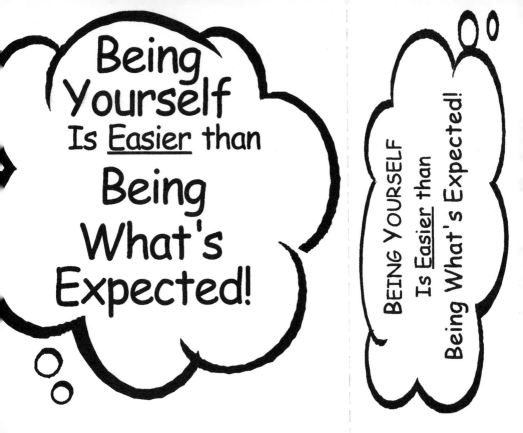

Reflections

HERE'S A THOUGHT!

MY MOTHER'S
PUBLISHING HOUSE

What

YOU DO

Is

WHAT'S

Remembered!

What YOU DO

Is What's

REMEMBERED!

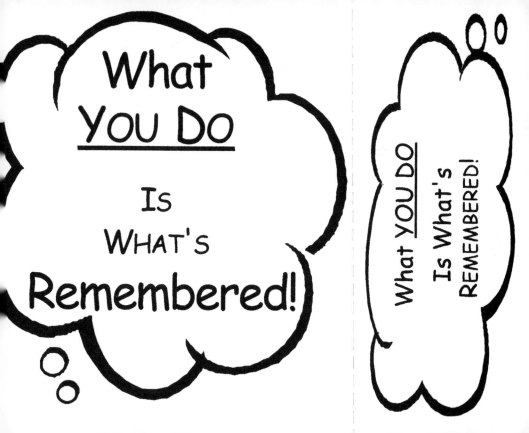

Reflections

HERE'S A THOUGHT!

MY MOTHER'S
PUBLISHING HOUSE

THE
CHANCE
Of A
Lifetime
Is Usually
Given Once!

THE
Chance Of A Lifetime
Is Usually Given Once!

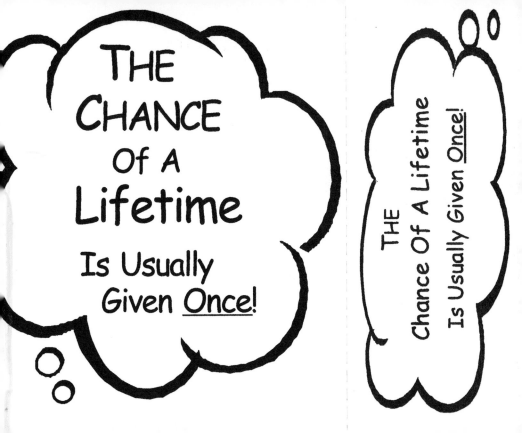

Reflections

HERE'S A THOUGHT!

MY MOTHER'S
PUBLISHING HOUSE

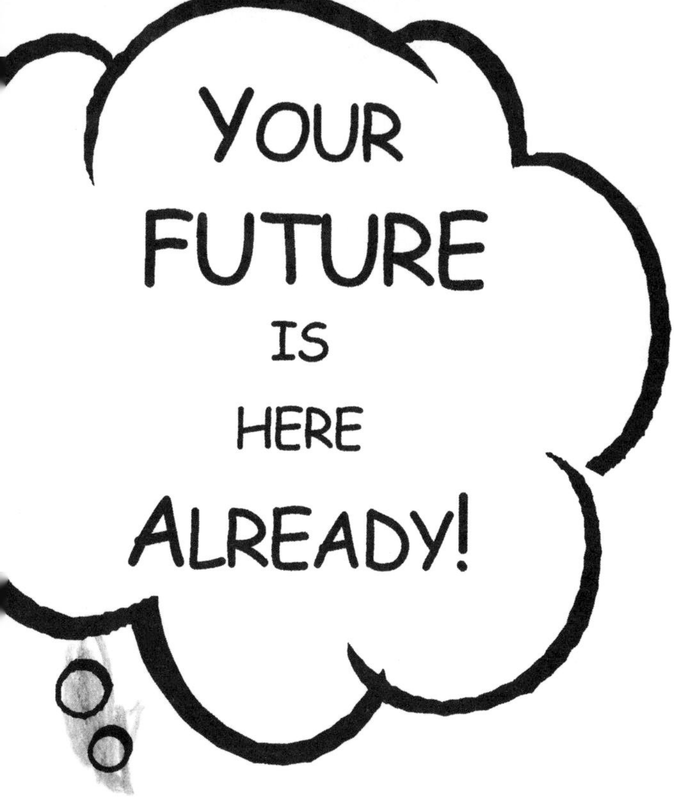
YOUR
FUTURE
IS
HERE
ALREADY!

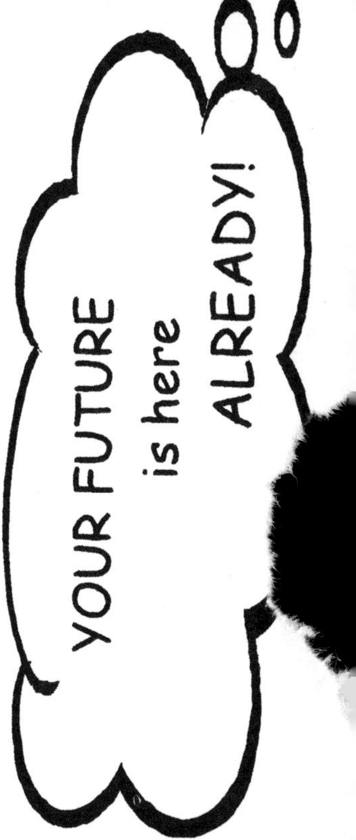
YOUR FUTURE
is here
ALREADY!

Reflections

HERE'S A THOUGHT!

MY MOTHER'S PUBLISHING

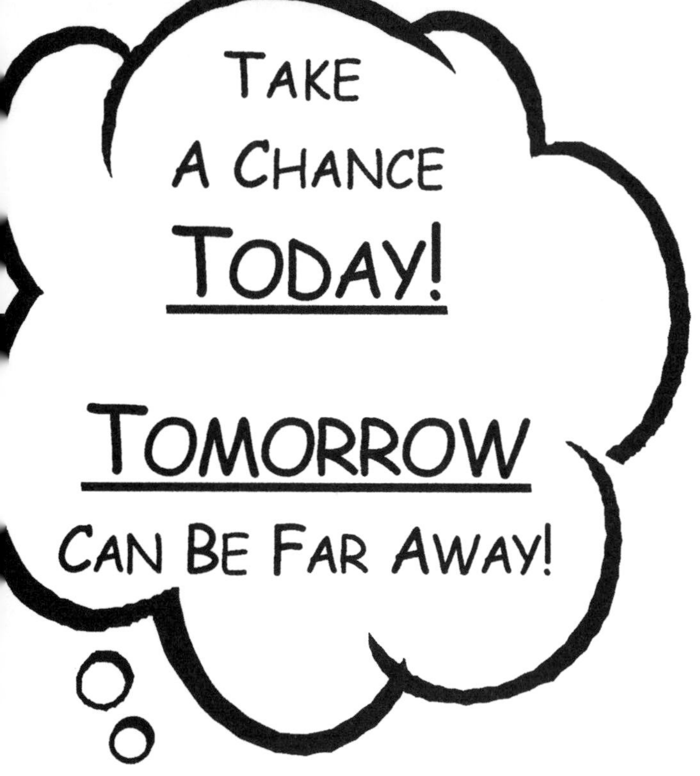
TAKE
A CHANCE
TODAY!
TOMORROW
CAN BE FAR AWAY!

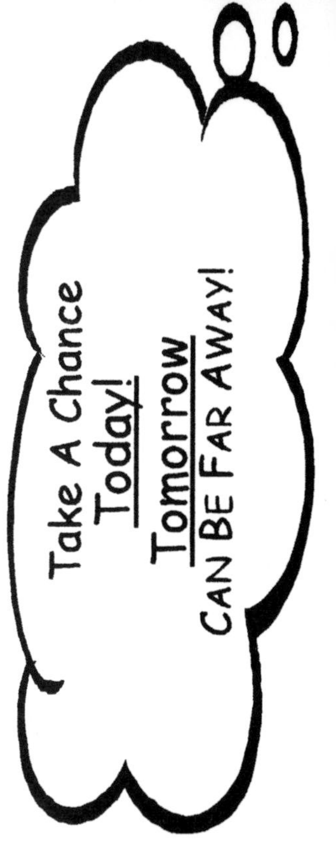
Take A Chance
Today!
Tomorrow
CAN BE FAR AWAY!

Reflections

HERE'S A THOUGHT!

MY MOTHER'S
PUBLISHING HOUSE

First Impressions

AREN'T NECESSARILY SO!

FIRST IMPRESSIONS AREN'T NECESSARILY SO!

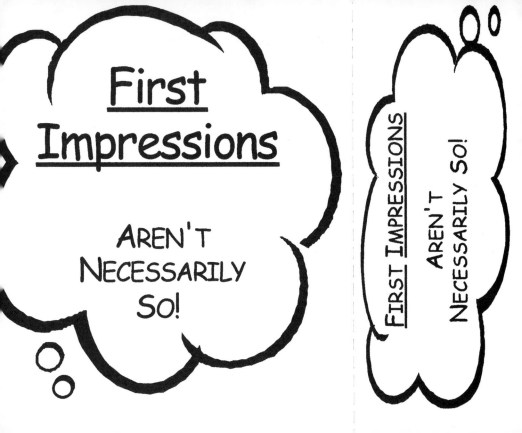

Reflections

HERE'S A THOUGHT!

MY MOTHER'S
PUBLISHING HOUSE

HOLDING YOUR GROUND

Means Holding
Your Own!

Holding Your Ground
Means
Holding Your Own!

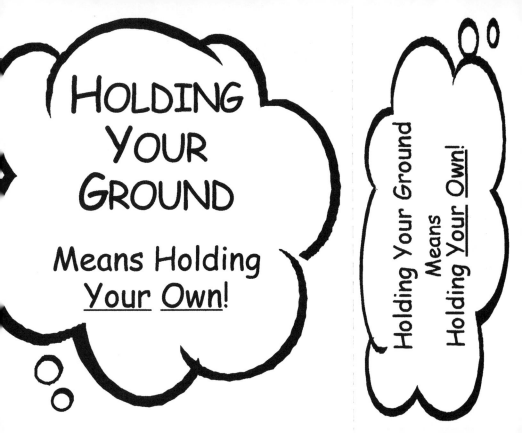

Reflections

HERE'S A THOUGHT!

MY MOTHER'S PUBLISHING HOUSE

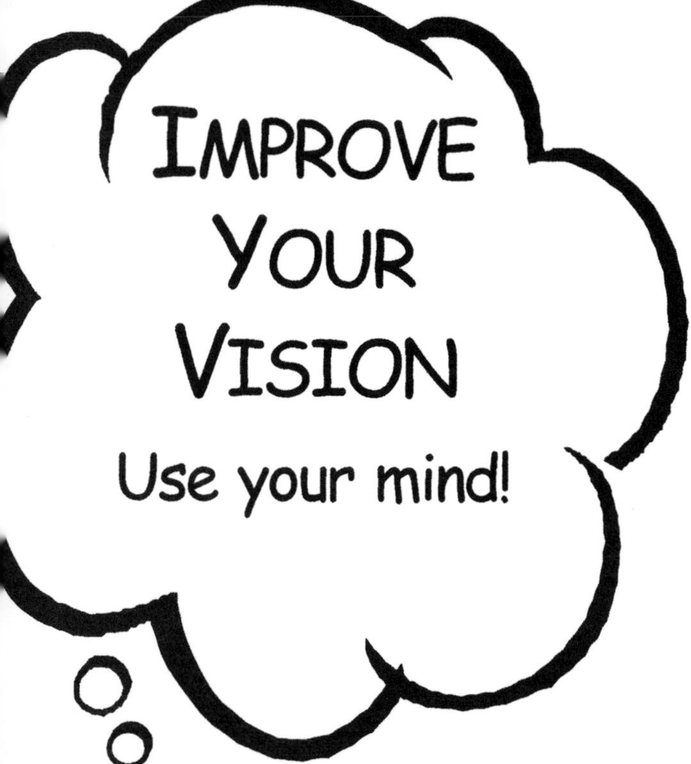
IMPROVE
YOUR
VISION
Use your mind!

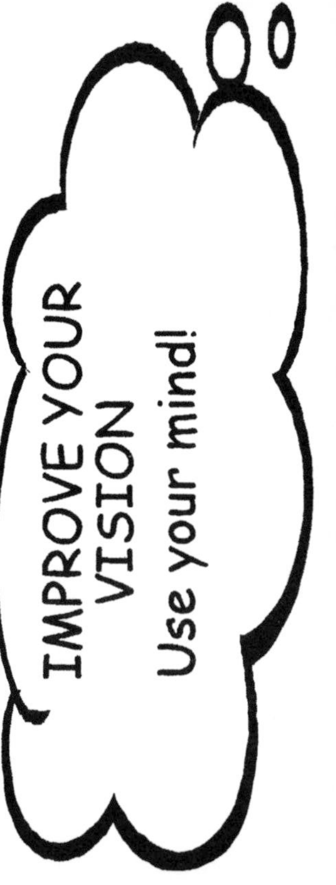
IMPROVE YOUR
VISION
Use your mind!

Reflections

HERE'S A THOUGHT!

MY MOTHER'S
PUBLISHING HOUSE

Be

Positive

In

Dealing With Others

<u>Your</u> <u>Best</u>

Will Show Through!

BE POSITIVE

In Dealing With Others

<u>YOUR</u> <u>BEST</u>

Will Show Through!

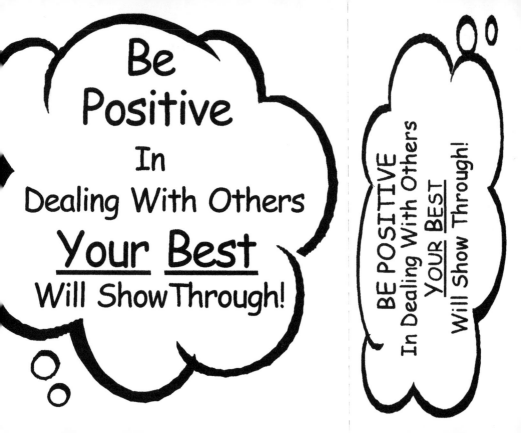

Reflections

HERE'S A THOUGHT!

MY MOTHER'S
PUBLISHING HOUSE

PUT

Your Life In His Hands

HE

<u>Never</u>

Lets Go!

Put

YOUR LIFE IN HIS HANDS

HE <u>Never</u> Lets Go!

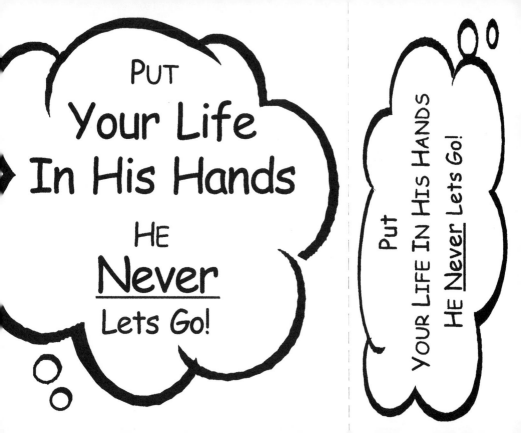

Reflections

HERE'S A THOUGHT!

MY MOTHER'S
PUBLISHING HOUSE

Remember
Everybody's
Good Points
and
They Will
Remember
Yours!

Remember Everybody's
GOOD POINTS
and they Will Remember Yours!

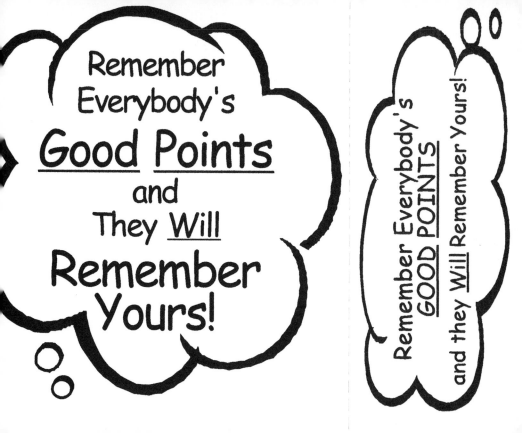

Reflections

HERE'S A THOUGHT!

MY MOTHER'S
PUBLISHING HOUSE

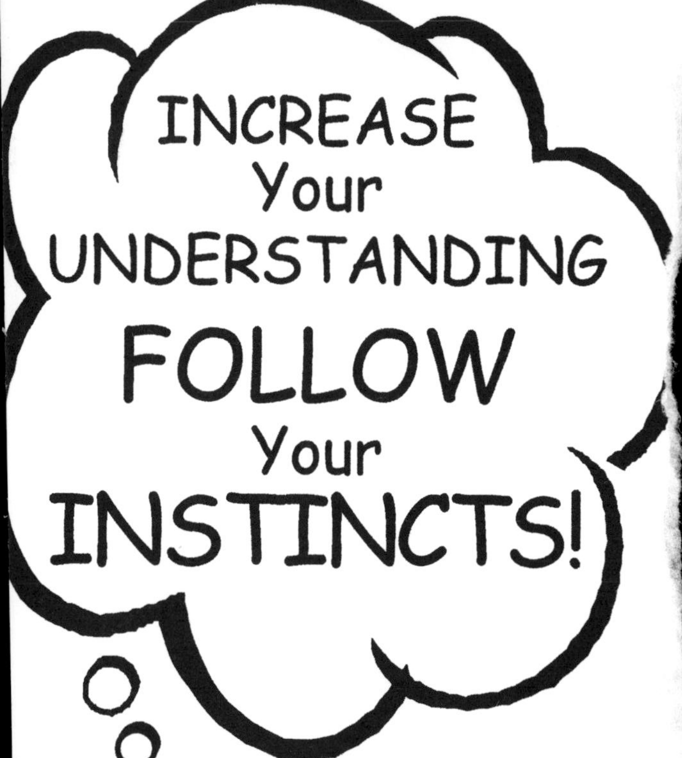
INCREASE
Your
UNDERSTANDING
FOLLOW
Your
INSTINCTS!

Reflections

BRING <u>BACK</u>
YOUR
Dreams and Desires

IT'S
<u>NEVER</u> TOO LATE TO
SUCCEED!

Bring Back Your
DREAMS AND DESIRES
It is <u>Never</u> Too Late to
SUCCEED!

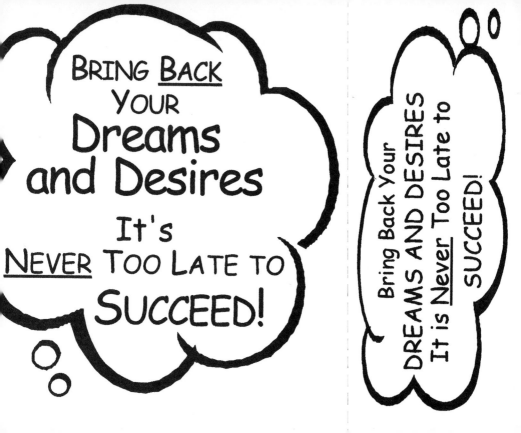

Reflections

HERE'S A THOUGHT!

MY MOTHER'S
PUBLISHING HOUSE

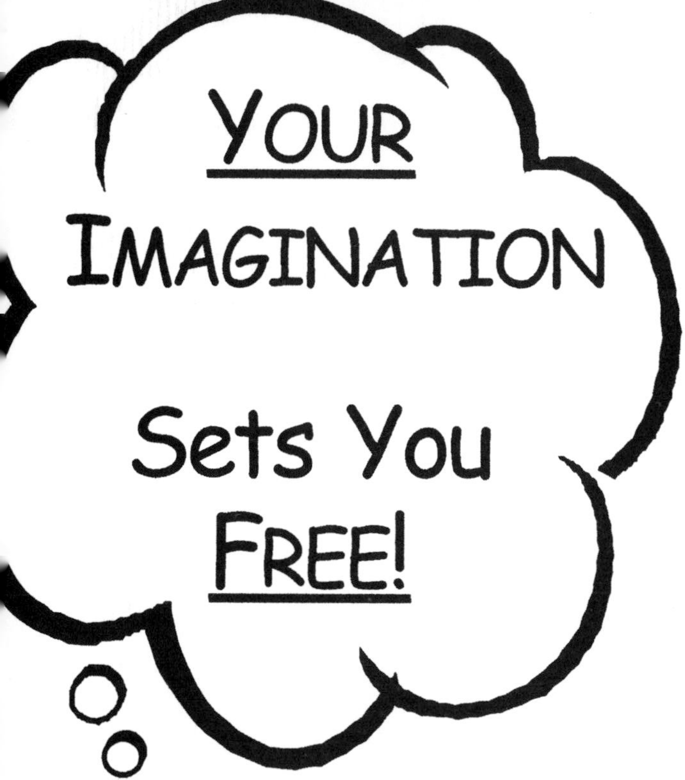
YOUR
IMAGINATION
Sets You
FREE!

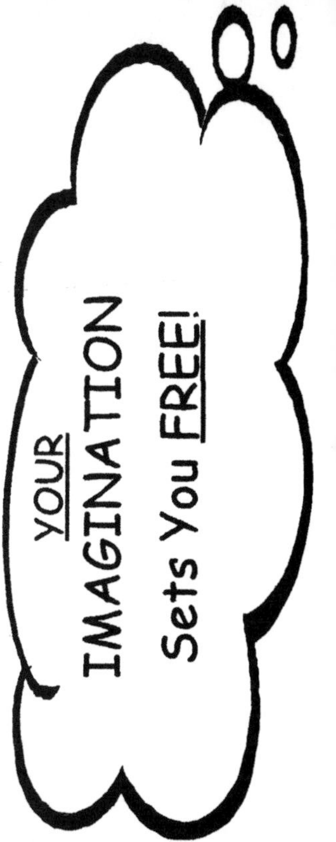
YOUR
IMAGINATION
Sets You FREE!

Reflections

HERE'S A THOUGHT!

MY MOTHER'S
PUBLISHING HOUSE

SEE

Your

Success

Morning, Noon, and Night!

See

YOUR SUCCESS

Morning, Noon, and Night!

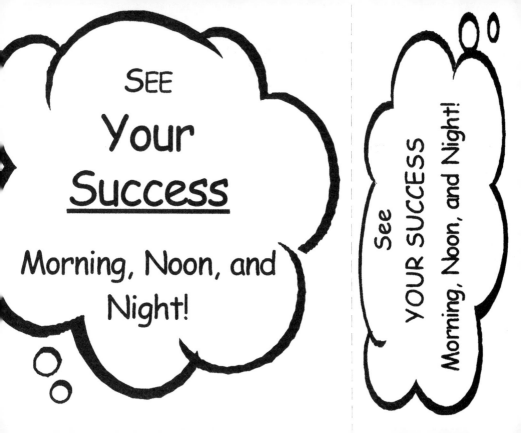

Reflections

HERE'S A THOUGHT!

MY MOTHER'S
PUBLISHING HOUSE

Great
Minds

Develop Through
Independent
Thinking!

GREAT MINDS
Develop Through
Independent Thinking!

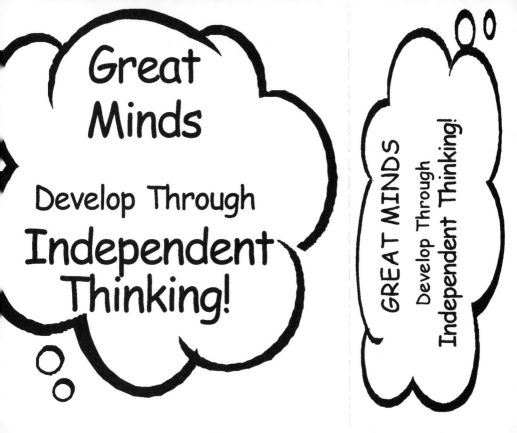

Reflections

HERE'S A THOUGHT!

MY MOTHER'S
PUBLISHING HOUSE

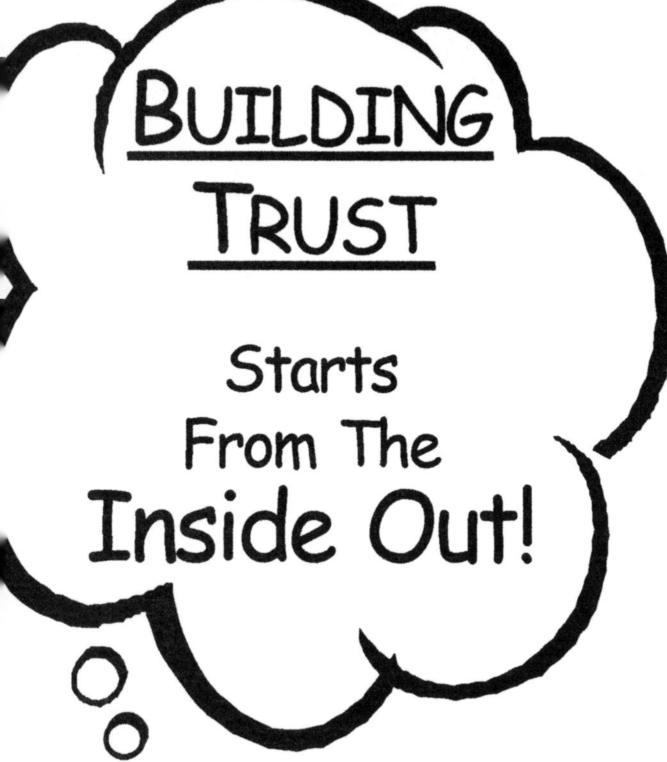
BUILDING
TRUST
Starts
From The
Inside Out!

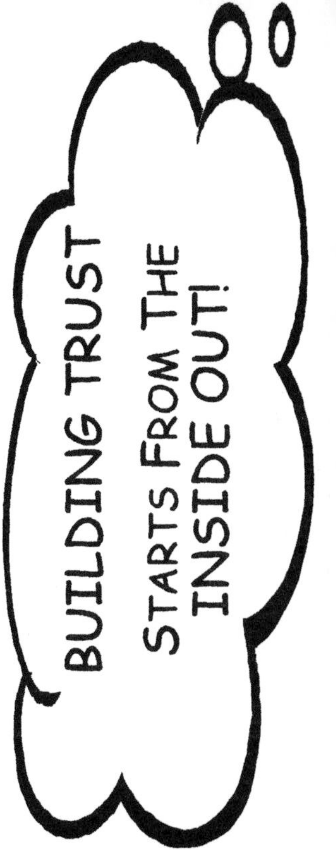
BUILDING TRUST
STARTS FROM THE
INSIDE OUT!

Reflections

HERE'S A THOUGHT!

MY MOTHER'S
PUBLISHING HOUSE

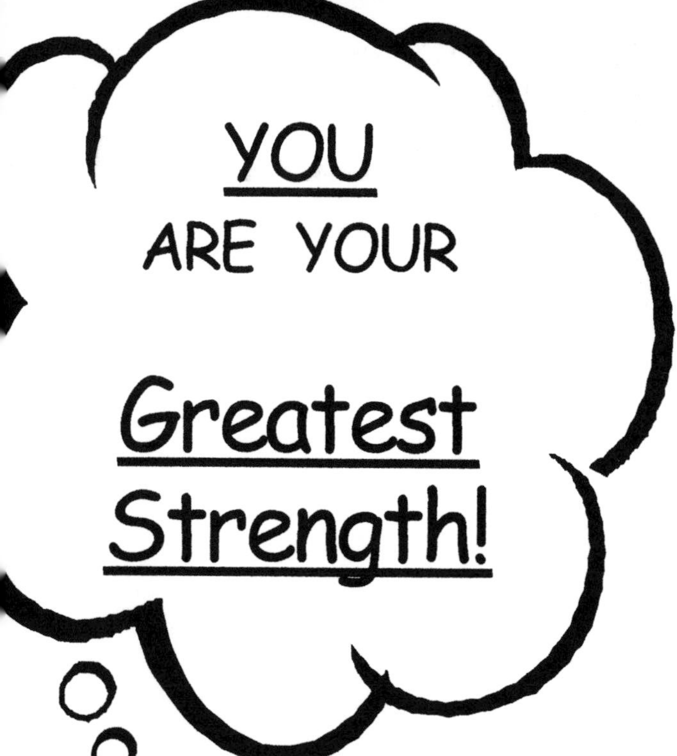
YOU
ARE YOUR
Greatest
Strength!

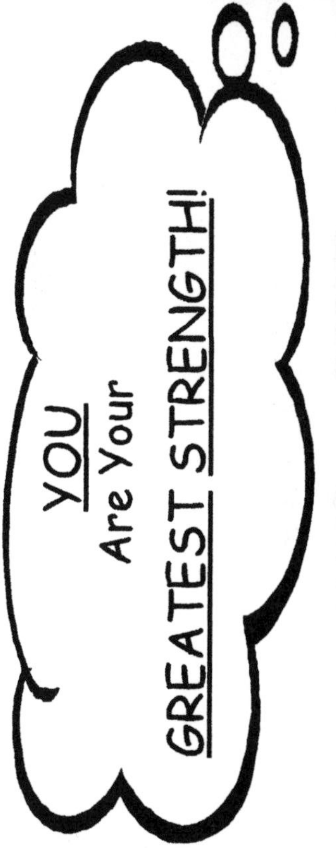
YOU
Are Your
GREATEST STRENGTH!

Reflections

HERE'S A THOUGHT!

MY MOTHER'S
PUBLISHING HOUSE

Open

A New Door

Step Into

The Future!

OPEN
A NEW DOOR
STEP INTO
THE FUTURE!

Reflections

HERE'S A THOUGHT!

MY MOTHER'S
PUBLISHING HOUSE

Discover
Something
That
No One Else Can
YOURSELF!

DISCOVER SOMETHING
That No One Else Can
YOURSELF!

Reflections

HERE'S A THOUGHT!

MY MOTHER'S
PUBLISHING HOUSE

Feeling Great, Feeling Fine...

You Can Do It All the Time!

Reflections

Finding
New Freedom
Means
Directing
Yourself!

FINDING
NEW FREEDOM
MEANS
DIRECTING YOURSELF!

Reflections

HERE'S A THOUGHT!

MY MOTHER'S
PUBLISHING HOUSE

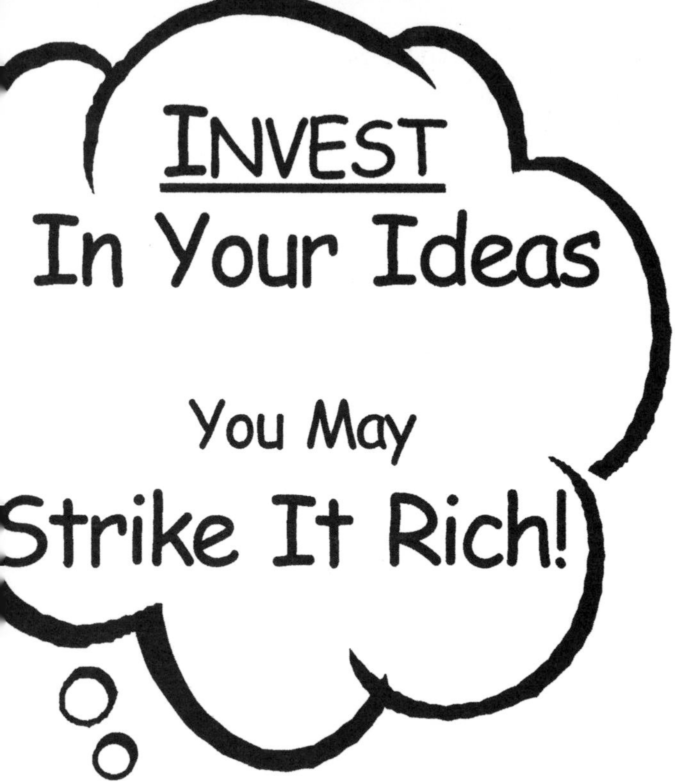
INVEST
In Your Ideas
You May
Strike It Rich!

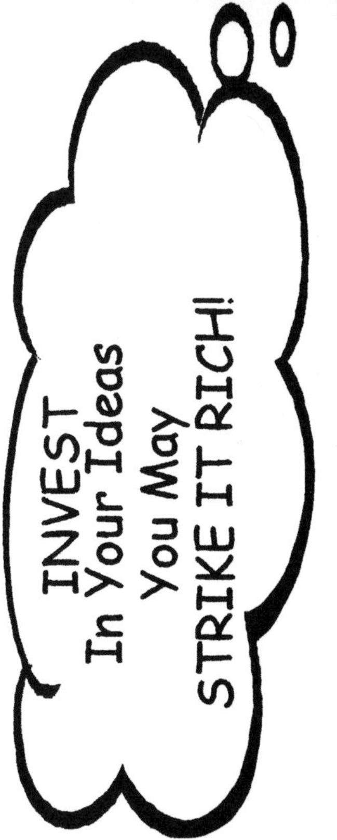
INVEST
In Your Ideas
You May
STRIKE IT RICH!

Reflections

HERE'S A THOUGHT!

MY MOTHER'S
PUBLISHING HOUSE

Put
Yourself First
But
Not Above
Others!

PUT
YOURSELF FIRST
BUT
NOT ABOVE OTHERS!

Reflections

HERE'S A THOUGHT!

MY MOTHER'S
PUBLISHING HOUSE

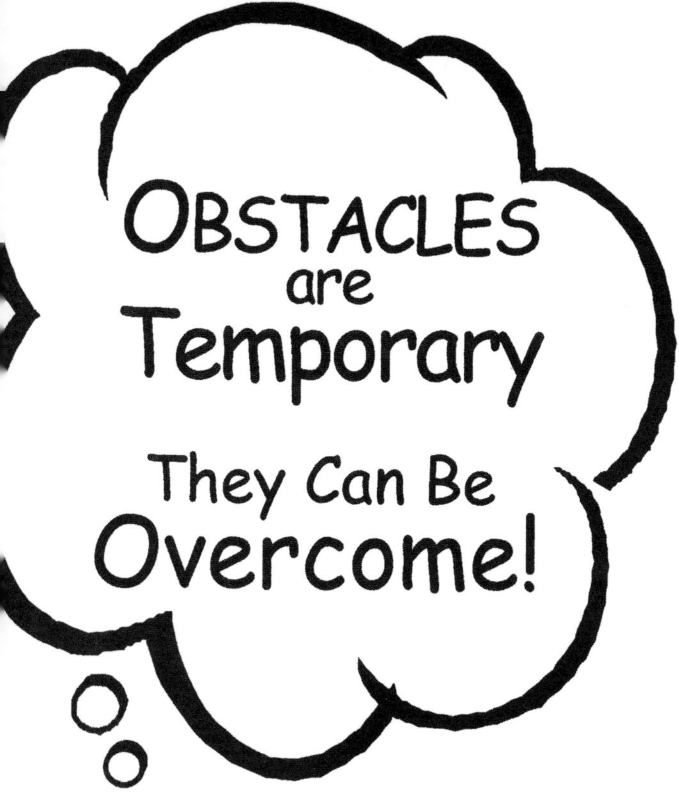
OBSTACLES
are
Temporary
They Can Be
Overcome!

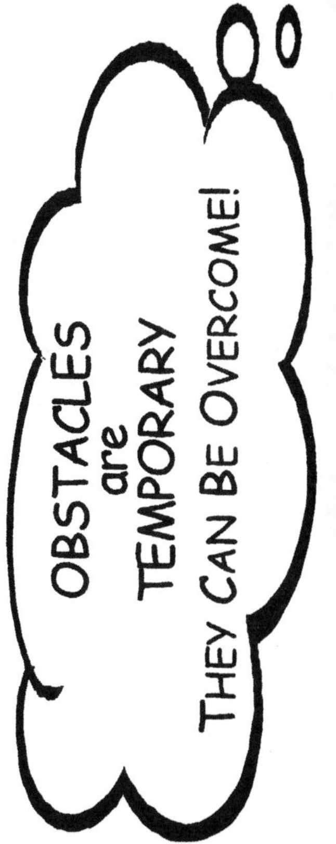
OBSTACLES
are
TEMPORARY
THEY CAN BE OVERCOME!

Reflections

HERE'S A THOUGHT!

MY MOTHER'S PUBLISHING HOUSE

Security

Starts
from Within and

Shows
Throughout
Your Life!

SECURITY
Starts from Within and
SHOWS
Throughout Your Life!

Reflections

HERE'S A THOUGHT!

MY MOTHER'S
PUBLISHING HOUSE

THE ROAD
To Heaven
Is Well Marked
Follow the Signs!

THE ROAD TO HEAVEN
IS WELL MARKED
FOLLOW THE SIGNS!

Reflections

HERE'S A THOUGHT!

MY MOTHER'S
PUBLISHING HOUSE

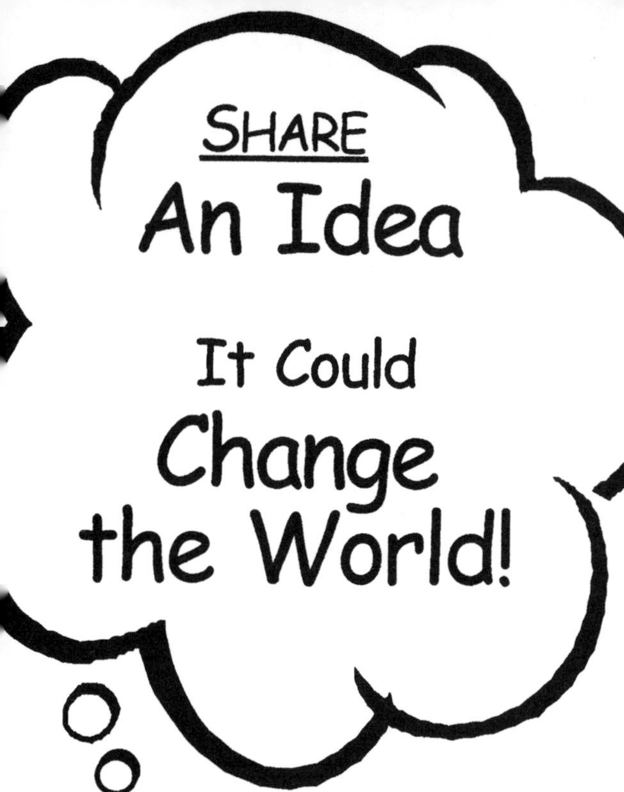
SHARE
An Idea
It Could
Change
the World!

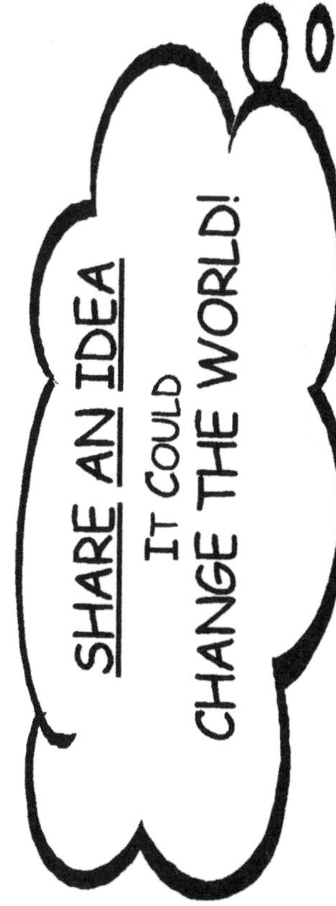
SHARE AN IDEA
IT COULD
CHANGE THE WORLD!

Reflections

HERE'S A THOUGHT!

MY MOTHER'S
PUBLISHING HOUSE

Think
with
<u>Wisdom</u>

Act
with
<u>Courage!</u>

<u>THINK</u> with <u>WISDOM</u>

<u>ACT</u> with <u>COURAGE!</u>

Reflections

HERE'S A THOUGHT!

MY MOTHER'S
PUBLISHING HOUSE

End an Argument Quickly

If Wrong, Admit It

If Not, Forget It!

End an Argument QUICKLY

If Wrong, ADMIT IT

If Not, FORGET IT!

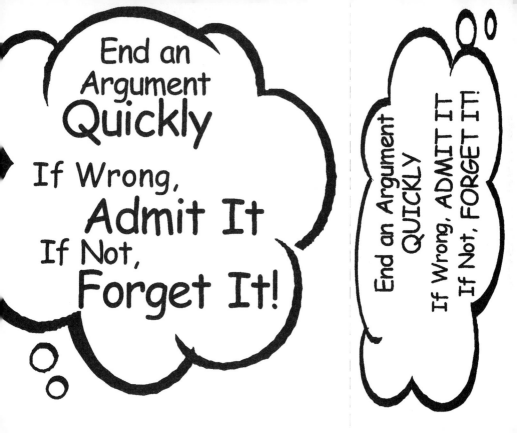

Reflections

HERE'S A THOUGHT!

MY MOTHER'S
PUBLISHING HOUSE

Don't

Carry A Grudge

The Weight

May

Break

Your Back!

DON'T

Carry A Grudge

THE WEIGHT

May Break Your Back!

Reflections

HERE'S A THOUGHT!

MY MOTHER'S
PUBLISHING HOUSE

Learning
From
The Past
Makes
The Present
An Easier Path!

LEARNING FROM THE PAST
MAKES THE PRESENT
An Easier Path!

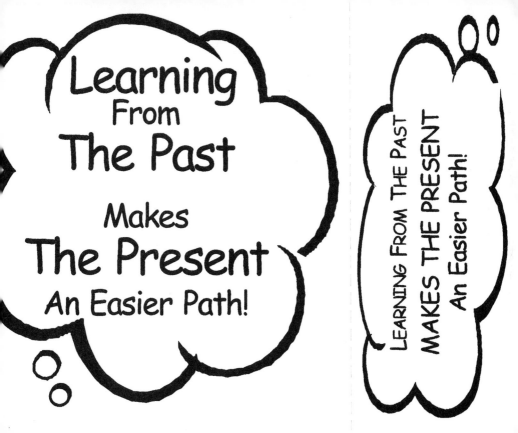

Reflections

HERE'S A THOUGHT!

MY MOTHER'S
PUBLISHING HOUSE

When
Making
COMMENTS

Be Constructive!

When Making COMMENTS
Be Constructive!

Reflections

HERE'S A THOUGHT!

MY MOTHER'S
PUBLISHING HOUSE

Stand Tall,
Hold Your Ground
Gently Bend,
Never Break!

STAND TALL,
HOLD YOUR GROUND
Gently Bend, Never Break!

Reflections

HERE'S A THOUGHT!

MY MOTHER'S
PUBLISHING HOUSE

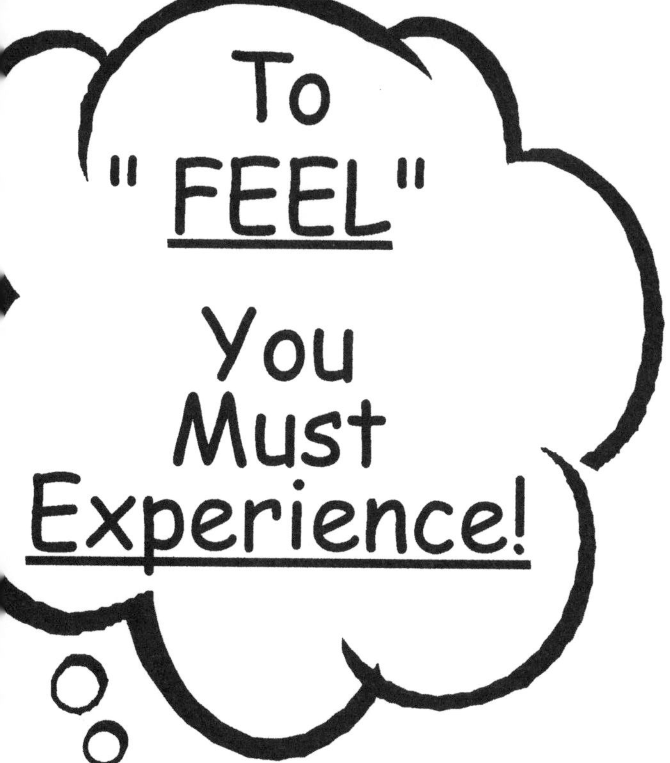
To
" FEEL "
You
Must
Experience!

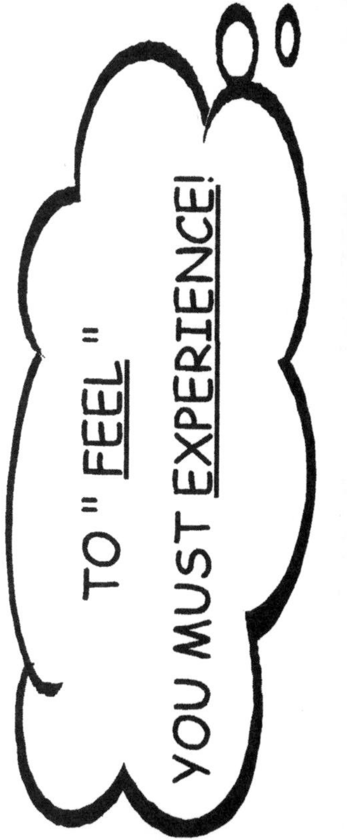
TO " FEEL "
YOU MUST EXPERIENCE!

Reflections

HERE'S A THOUGHT!

MY MOTHER'S
PUBLISHING HOUSE

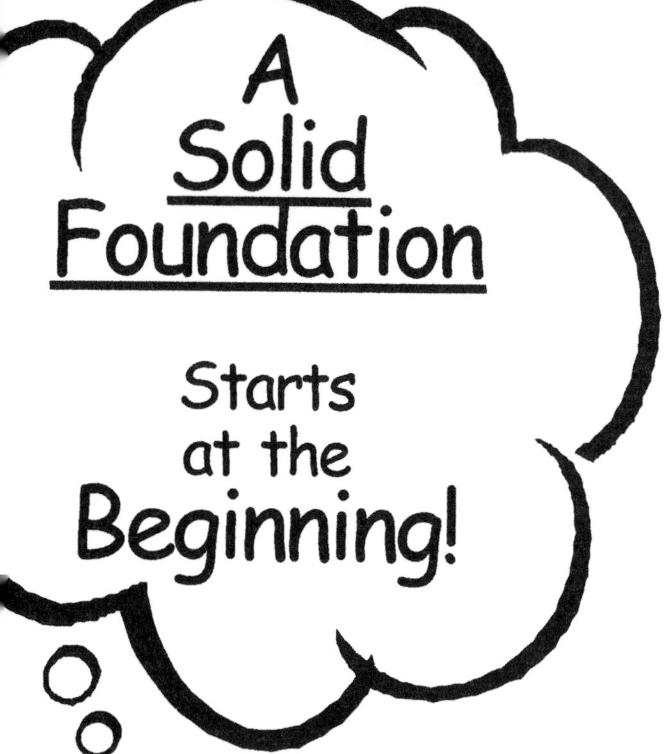
A
Solid
Foundation
Starts
at the
Beginning!

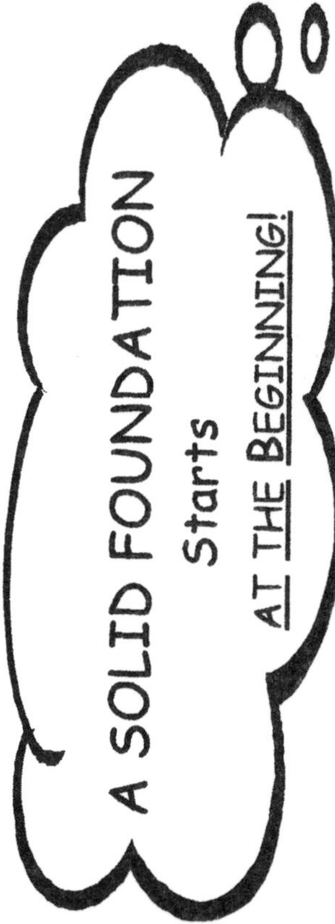
A SOLID FOUNDATION
Starts
AT THE BEGINNING!

Reflections

HERE'S A THOUGHT!

MY MOTHER'S
PUBLISHING HOUSE

Do the
Possible

Give
The
Impossible
A Little More Time!

Do the Possible
GIVE THE IMPOSSIBLE
A Little More Time!

Reflections

HERE'S A THOUGHT!

MY MOTHER'S
PUBLISHING HOUSE

People
Draw
To
Themselves

What They
Project
To OTHERS!

People Draw To Themselves
WHAT THEY PROJECT
To Others!

Reflections

HERE'S A THOUGHT!

MY MOTHER'S
PUBLISHING HOUSE

STRENGTHEN

Your Mind

BUILD ON

Healthy, Positive Thoughts!

STRENGTHEN YOUR MIND
BUILD ON
HEALTHY, POSITIVE
THOUGHTS!

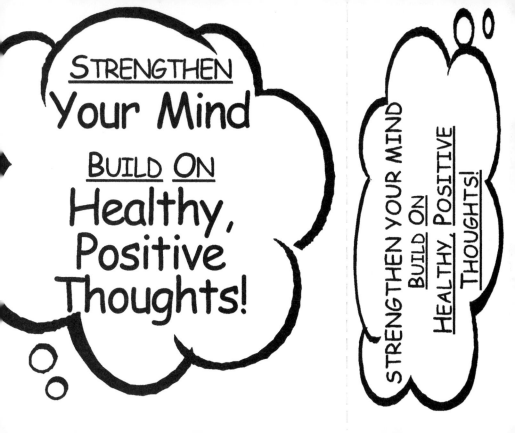

Reflections

HERE'S A THOUGHT!

MY MOTHER'S
PUBLISHING HOUSE

Answer Questions As If <u>YOU</u> Were Asking Them!

ANSWER QUESTIONS As If <u>YOU</u> WERE ASKING THEM!

Reflections

HERE'S A THOUGHT!

MY MOTHER'S
PUBLISHING HOUSE

If You

Wouldn't

Say It

About Yourself

Refrain

From Saying It
About Others!

If You Wouldn't
SAY IT ABOUT YOURSELF
Refrain From
SAYING IT ABOUT OTHERS!

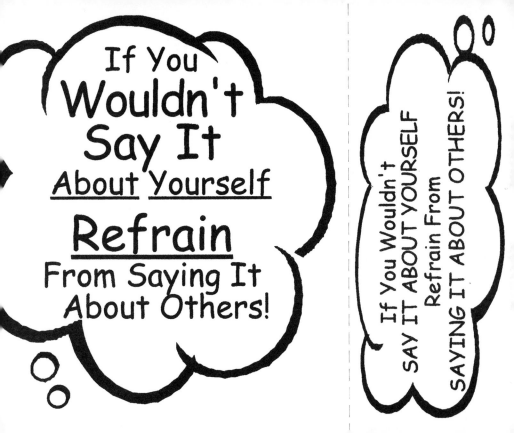

Reflections

HERE'S A THOUGHT!

MY MOTHER'S
PUBLISHING HOUSE

OTHERS

MAY ASK FOR

YOUR HELP

BE PREPARED!

OTHERS MAY ASK FOR
YOUR HELP
BE PREPARED!

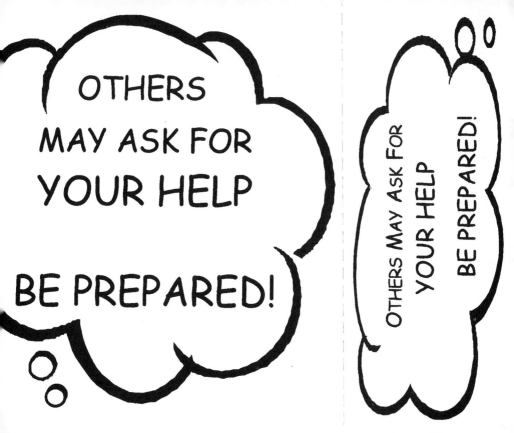

Reflections

HERE'S A THOUGHT!

MY MOTHER'S
PUBLISHING HOUSE

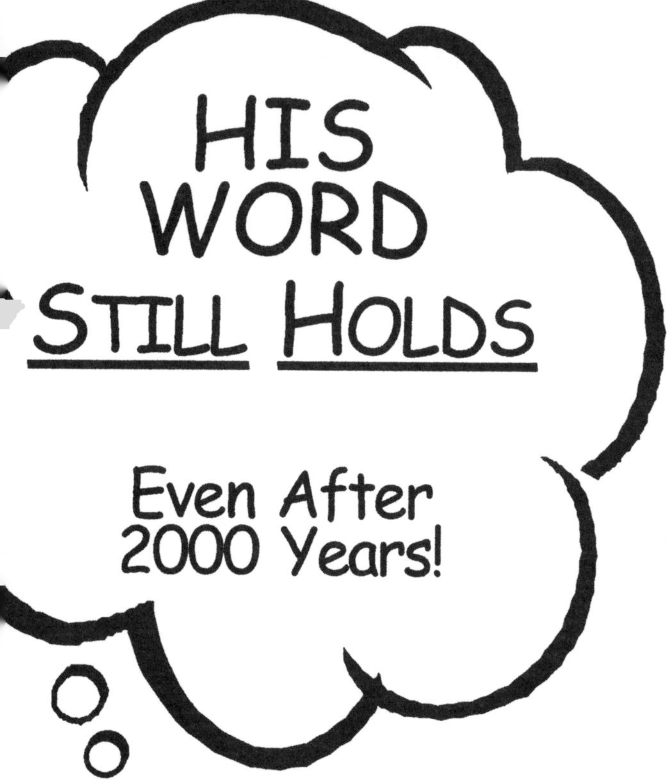
HIS
WORD
STILL HOLDS
Even After
2000 Years!

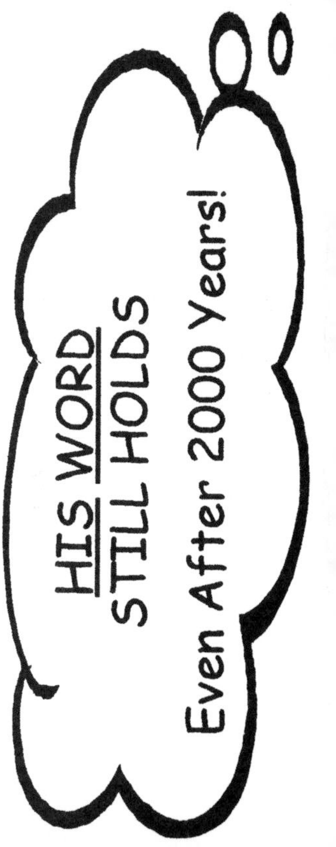
HIS WORD
STILL HOLDS
Even After 2000 Years!

Reflections

HERE'S A THOUGHT!

MY MOTHER'S
PUBLISHING HOUSE

Plan
For
Excellence

BE YOUR BEST
Everyday!

PLAN FOR EXCELLENCE
Be Your Best
EVERYDAY!

Reflections

HERE'S A THOUGHT!

MY MOTHER'S
PUBLISHING HOUSE

FIND YOUR SUCCESS

Keep Company

WITH IT!

FIND YOUR SUCCESS
Keep Company With It!

Reflections

HERE'S A THOUGHT!

MY MOTHER'S PUBLISHING HOUSE

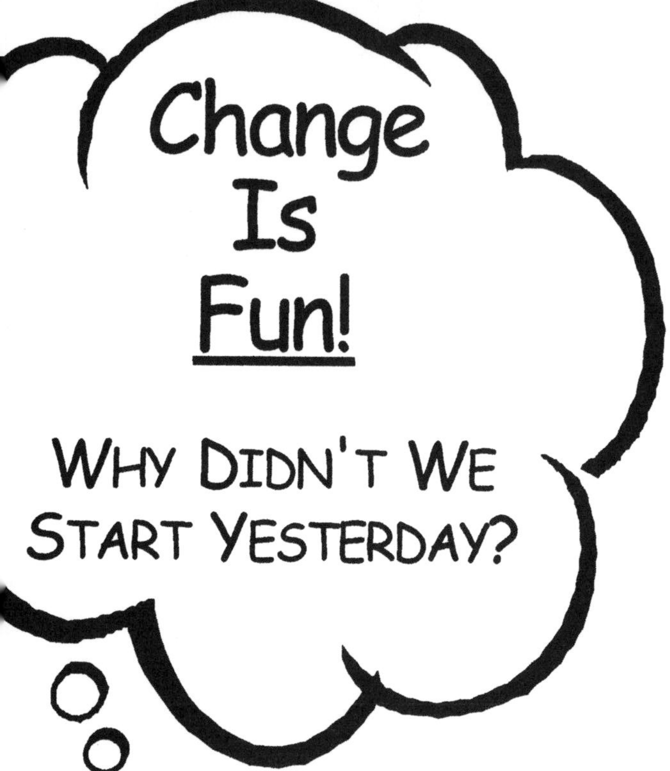
Change
Is
Fun!
WHY DIDN'T WE
START YESTERDAY?

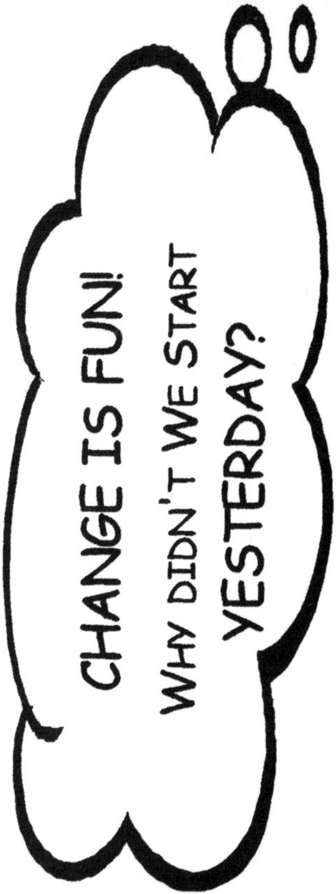
CHANGE IS FUN!
WHY DIDN'T WE START
YESTERDAY?

Reflections

HERE'S A THOUGHT!

MY MOTHER'S PUBLISHING HOUSE

RELAX

Your Mind
Controls
Your Body!

RELAX

YOUR MIND
CONTROLS YOUR BODY!

Reflections

HERE'S A THOUGHT!

MY MOTHER'S
PUBLISHING HOUSE

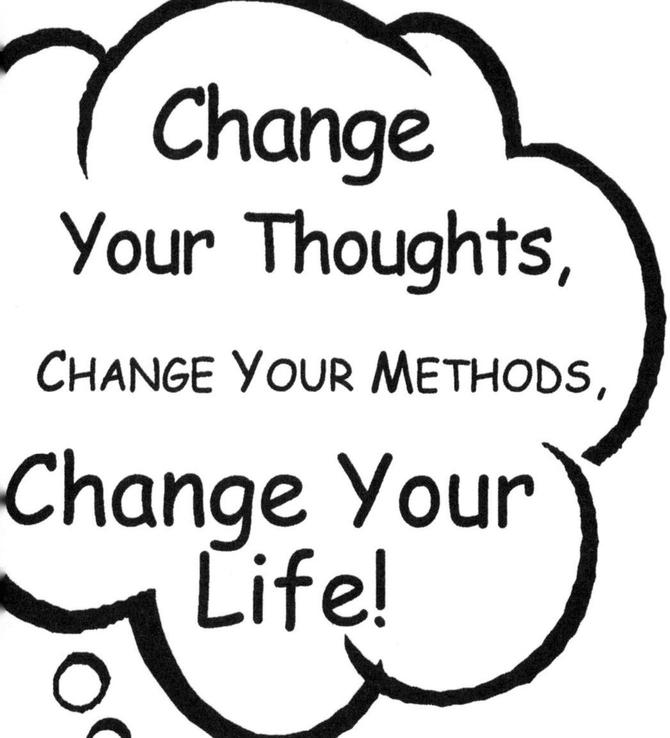
Change
Your Thoughts,
Change Your Methods,
Change Your
Life!

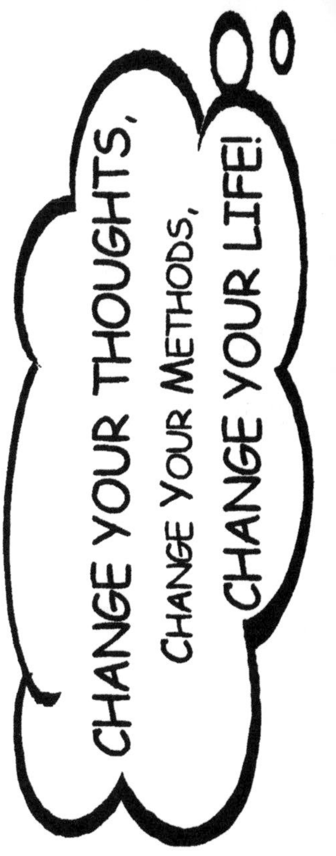
Change Your Thoughts,
Change Your Methods,
Change Your Life!

Reflections

HERE'S A THOUGHT!

MY MOTHER'S
PUBLISHING HOUSE

Take Time To

<u>TREAT</u>

YOURSELF

Special...

and

YOU WILL BE!

TAKE TIME

TO <u>TREAT</u> YOURSELF

SPECIAL

<u>AND</u> <u>YOU</u> <u>WILL</u> <u>BE!</u>

Reflections

HERE'S A THOUGHT!

MY MOTHER'S
PUBLISHING HOUSE

When your

Life's Path

Is Blocked

<u>REMEMBER</u>

There's

Another Way!

When Your

<u>LIFE'S PATH</u>

is Blocked

<u>REMEMBER:</u> There's

Another Way!

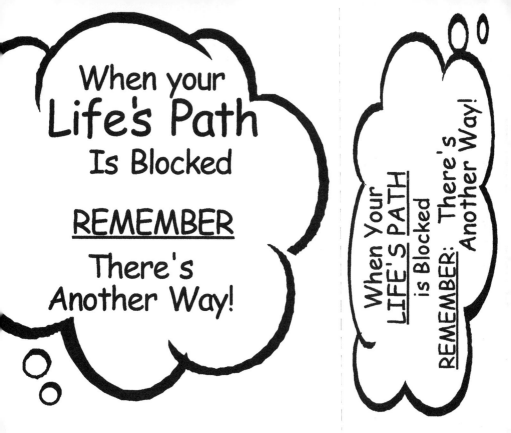

Reflections

HERE'S A THOUGHT!

MY MOTHER'S
PUBLISHING HOUSE

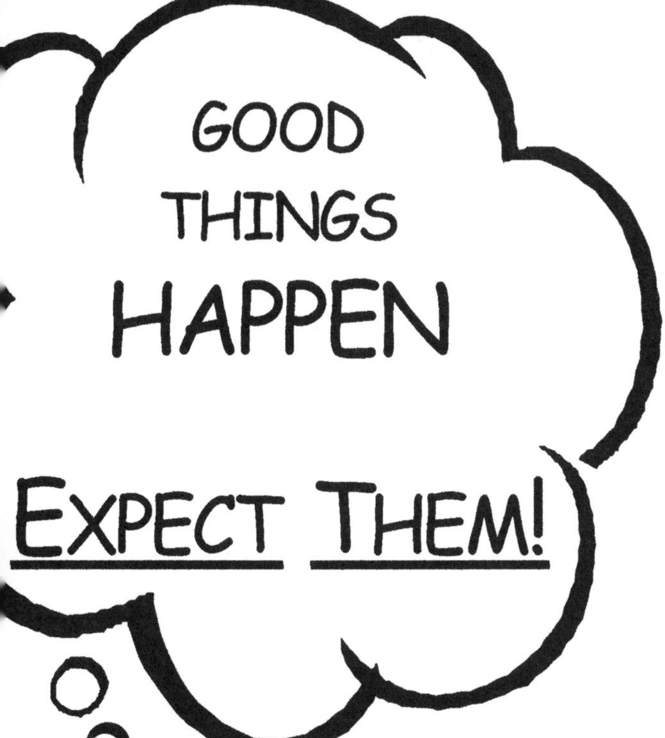
GOOD
THINGS
HAPPEN
EXPECT THEM!

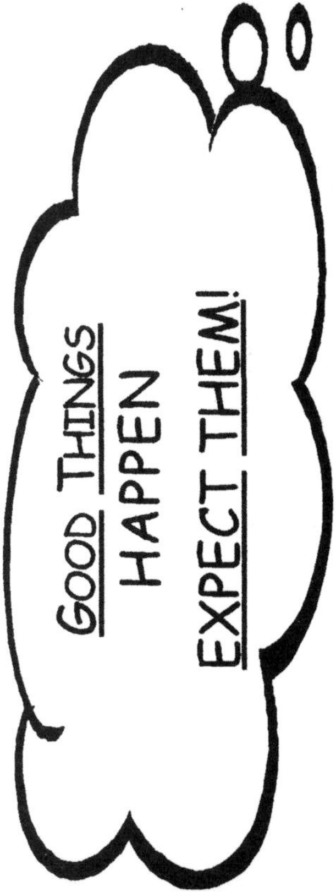
GOOD THINGS
HAPPEN
EXPECT THEM!

Reflections

HERE'S A THOUGHT!

MY MOTHER'S
PUBLISHING HOUSE

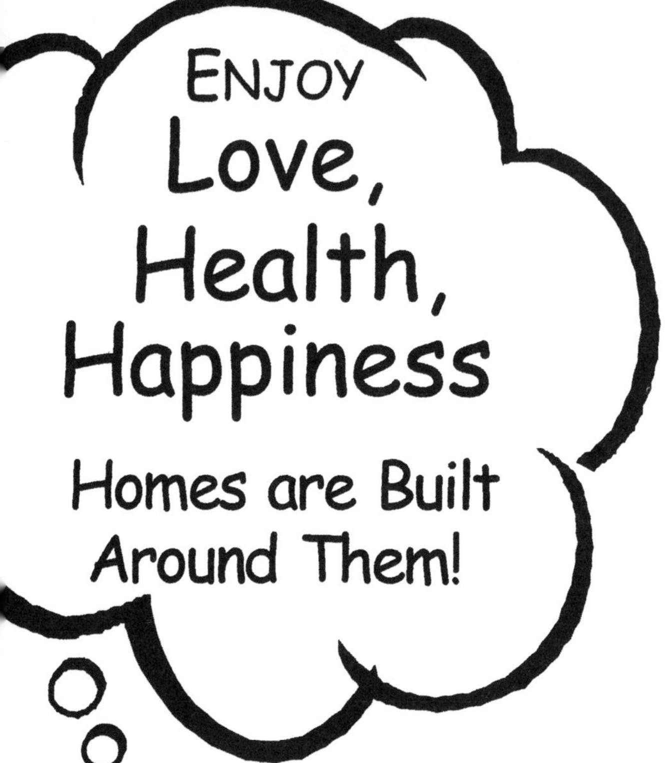
ENJOY
Love,
Health,
Happiness
Homes are Built
Around Them!

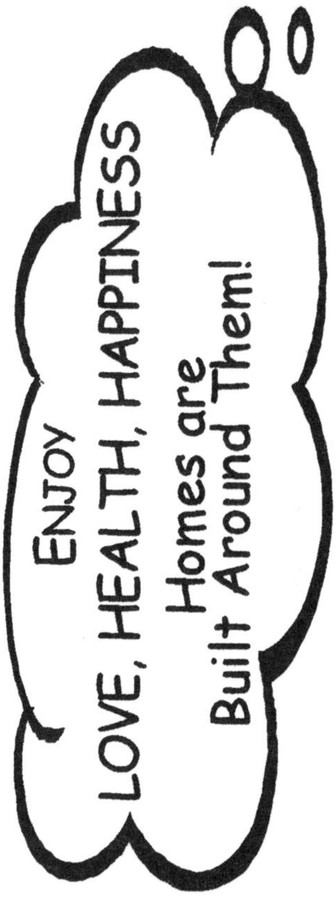
ENJOY
LOVE, HEALTH, HAPPINESS
Homes are
Built Around Them!

Reflections

HERE'S A THOUGHT!

MY MOTHER'S
PUBLISHING HOUSE

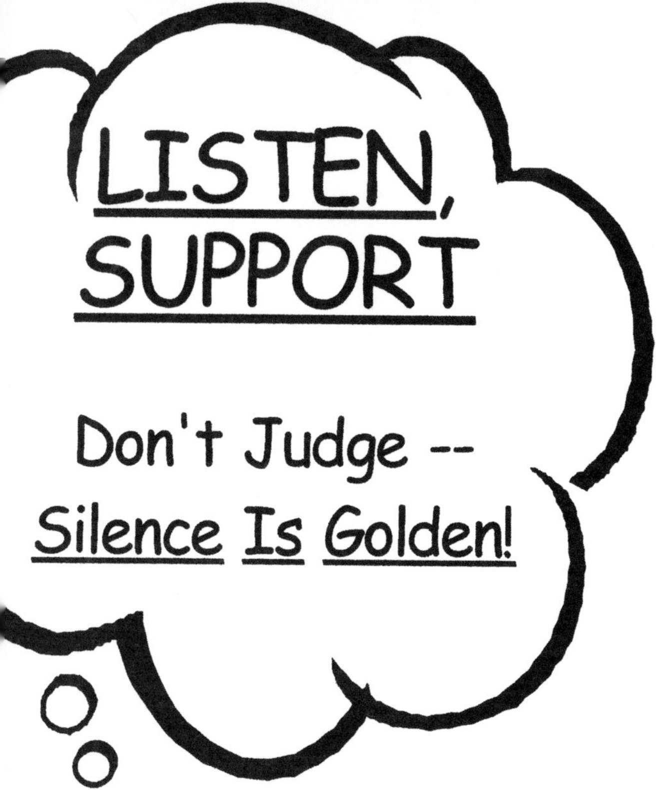
LISTEN,
SUPPORT
Don't Judge --
Silence Is Golden!

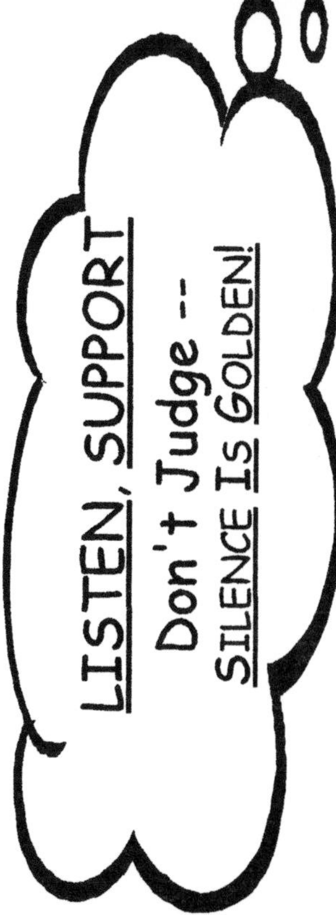
LISTEN, SUPPORT
Don't Judge --
SILENCE IS GOLDEN!

Reflections

HERE'S A THOUGHT!

MY MOTHER'S
PUBLISHING HOUSE

THE
FIRST
STEP
In
MAKING FRIENDS
Is Being One!

THE FIRST STEP
In Making Friends
IS BEING ONE!

Reflections

HERE'S A THOUGHT!

MY MOTHER'S
PUBLISHING HOUSE

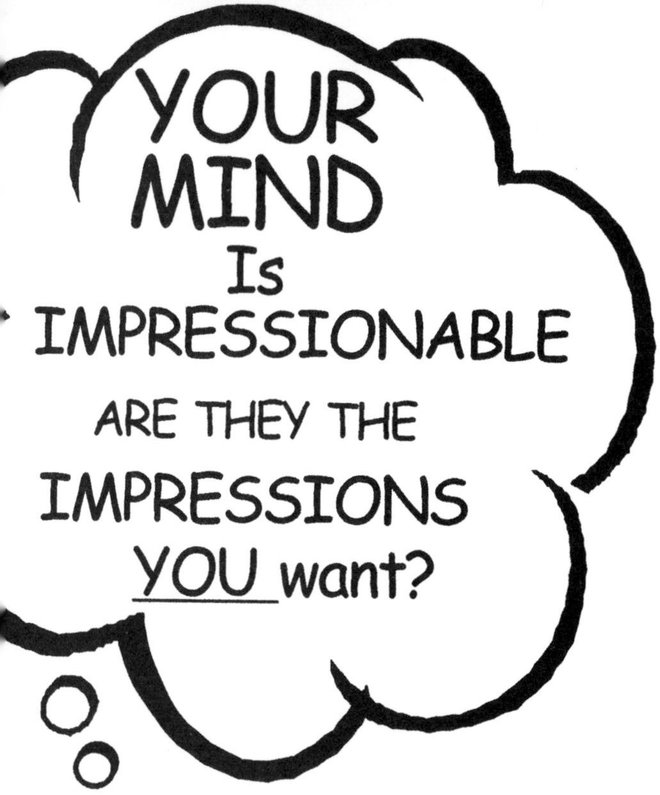
YOUR
MIND
Is
IMPRESSIONABLE
ARE THEY THE
IMPRESSIONS
YOU want?

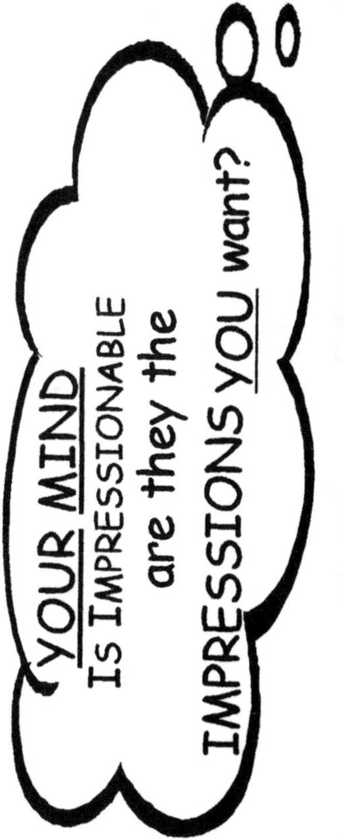
YOUR MIND
Is IMPRESSIONABLE
are they the
IMPRESSIONS YOU want?

Reflections

HERE'S A THOUGHT!

MY MOTHER'S
PUBLISHING HOUSE

SMILE

When You
See
OTHERS

THEY WILL
LOOK FORWARD
To Seeing You!

SMILE
WHEN YOU SEE OTHERS
THEY WILL
Look Forward To Seeing You!

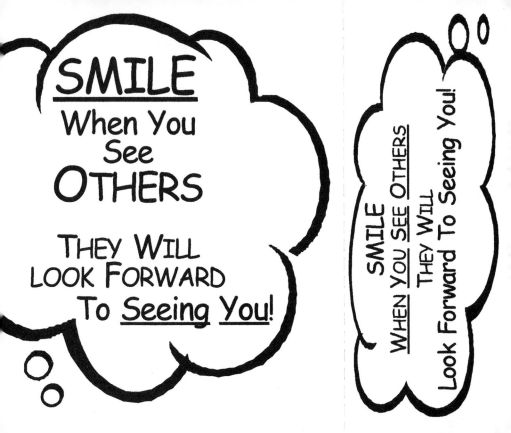

Reflections

HERE'S A THOUGHT!

MY MOTHER'S
PUBLISHING HOUSE

When
You
Go The
Extra Mile

You Are
Already
Ahead!

WHEN YOU
GO THE EXTRA MILE
You Are Already Ahead!

Reflections

HERE'S A THOUGHT!

MY MOTHER'S
PUBLISHING HOUSE

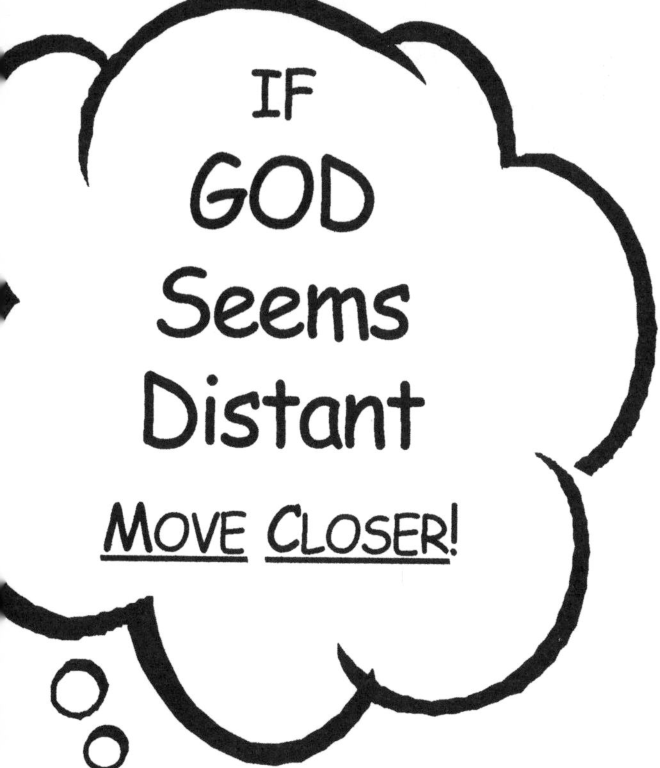
IF
GOD
Seems
Distant
MOVE CLOSER!

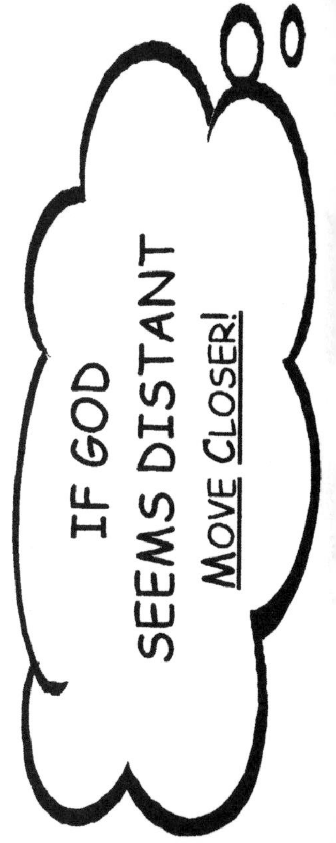
IF GOD
SEEMS DISTANT
MOVE CLOSER!

Reflections

HERE'S A THOUGHT!

MY MOTHER'S
PUBLISHING HOUSE

THERE IS

ALWAYS

A

BETTER

WAY

Find It!

THERE IS

ALWAYS

A BETTER WAY

Find it!

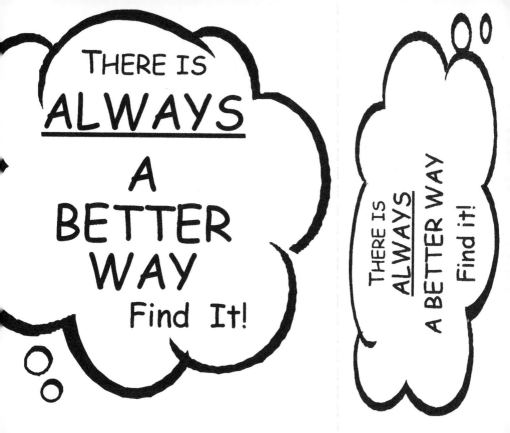

Reflections

HERE'S A THOUGHT!

MY MOTHER'S
PUBLISHING HOUSE

OPPORTUNITY

is

available

EVERYDAY!

Be Ready For It!

OPPORTUNITY IS available EVERYDAY!

Be ready for it!

Reflections

HERE'S A THOUGHT!

MY MOTHER'S
PUBLISHING HOUSE

HOW MUCH
Can you
GET
OUT OF LIFE?
As Much As
You Put Into It!

HOW MUCH
CAN YOU GET OUT OF LIFE?
As Much As You Put Into It!

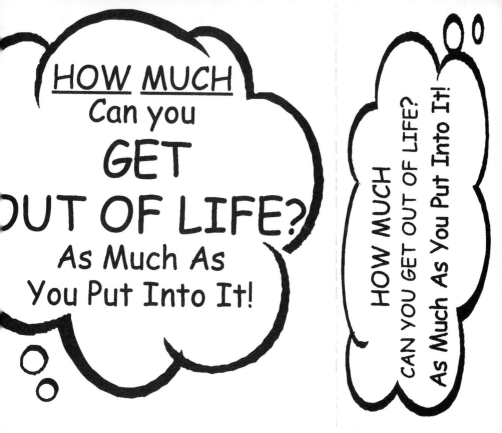

Reflections

HERE'S A THOUGHT!

MY MOTHER'S PUBLISHING HOUSE

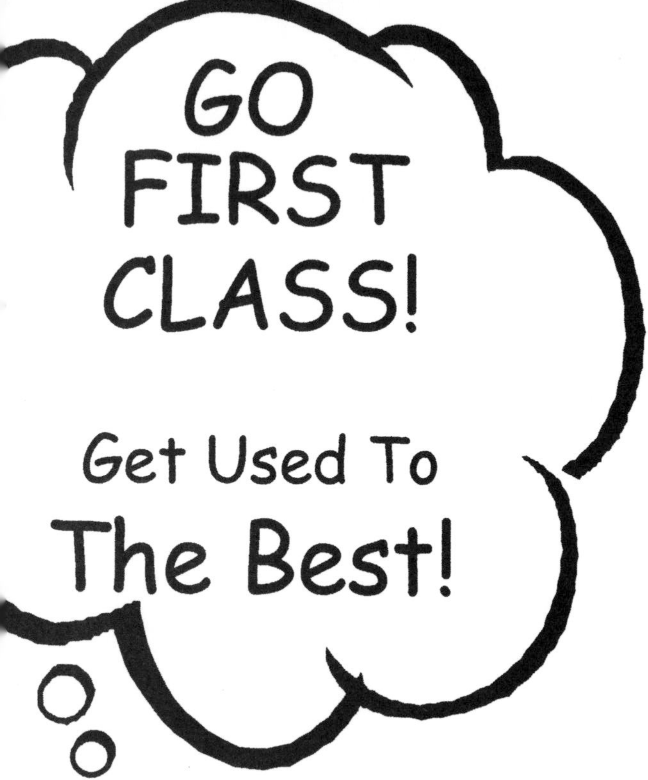
GO
FIRST
CLASS!
Get Used To
The Best!

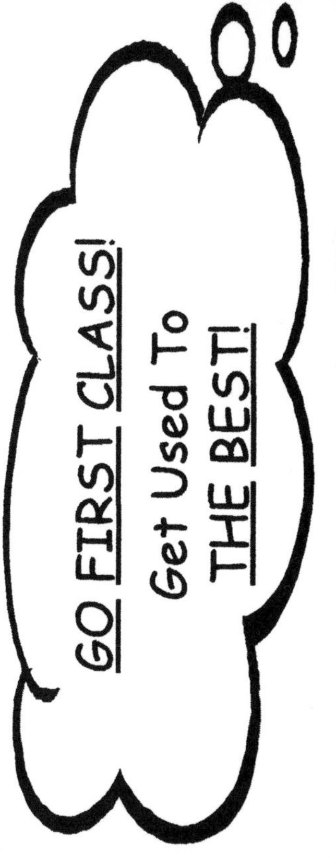
GO FIRST CLASS!
Get Used To
THE BEST!

Reflections

HERE'S A THOUGHT!

MY MOTHER'S
PUBLISHING HOUSE

Want It,
Develop It
and
YOU WILL
Have It!

WANT IT, DEVELOP IT
and
YOU WILL
HAVE IT!

Reflections

HERE'S A THOUGHT!

MY MOTHER'S
PUBLISHING HOUSE

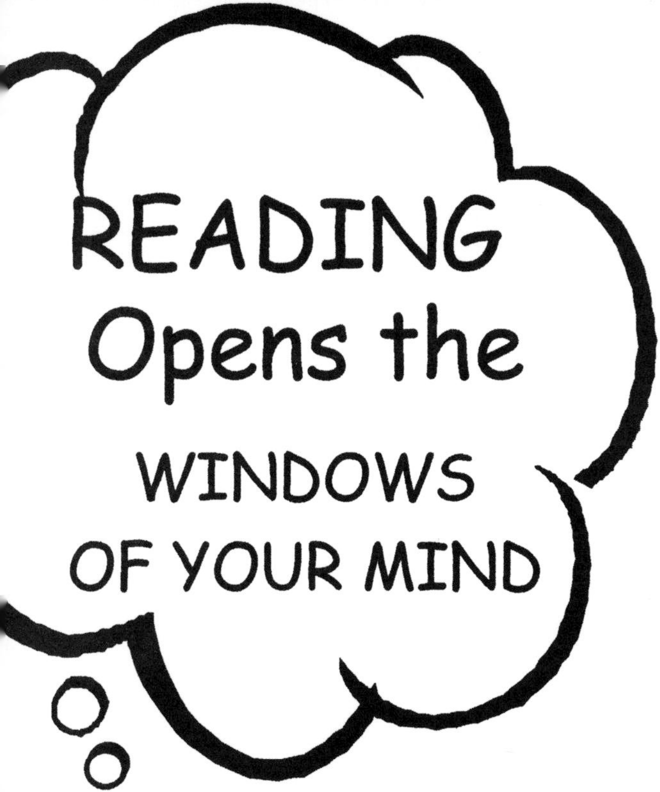
READING
Opens the
WINDOWS
OF YOUR MIND

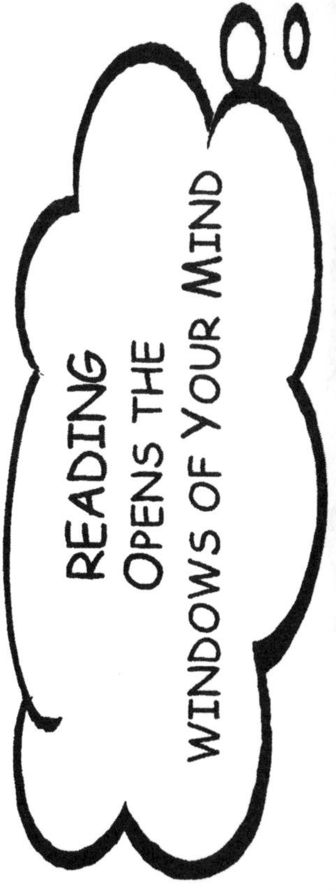
READING
OPENS THE
WINDOWS OF YOUR MIND

Reflections

HERE'S A THOUGHT!

MY MOTHER'S
PUBLISHING HOUSE

KEEP

Your MIND OPEN,
Your BODY MOVING

and your
SPIRIT
SOARING!

KEEP YOUR
MIND OPEN
YOUR BODY MOVING,
AND
YOUR SPIRIT SOARING!

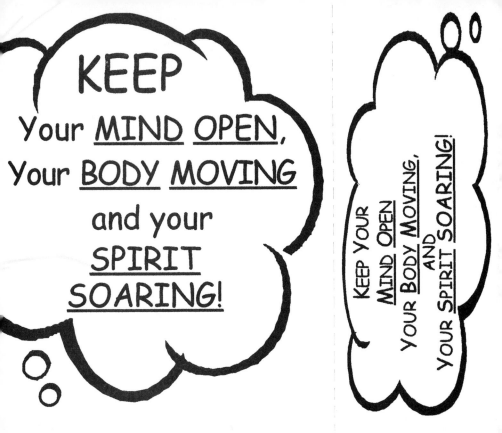

**MY MOTHER'S
PUBLISHING HOUSE**

23933 Eureka Road
Taylor, MI 48180
Phone: (734) 287-2930
FAX: (734) 287-7788

ABOUT THE AUTHOR

Norm Caldwell, Director
ACHIEVE NOW INSTITUTE

After successfully completing his tour of duty in
military, Norm became interested in Psycholog
which sparked his interest in helping others ar
ultimately led him to the study of the mind. H
attended the State Licensed Hypnotism Traini
Institute of Los Angeles, with Director Gill Boy

Norm's successfully proven techniques of
Hypnotherapy have helped thousands of clients re
stress, lose weight, stop smoking, and
increase confidence.

As an author, teacher, and radio/television person
Norm has had the opportunity to touch the lives
many people implementing meaningful
improvements. He has dedicated the last 15 yea
his life to helping people by sharing
techniques that work!

YOU CAN TAKE CONTROL OF YOUR LIF

DYNAMIC SELF-ENRICHMENT AUDIO CASSETTES

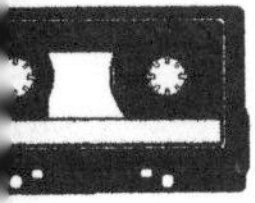

BREAK AWAY SERIES

Break away from SMOKING

Break away from STRESS!

k away from FAT!

IMPROVE your Concentration!

IMPROVE your Memory!

PROVE your Health!

Break away from ALCOHOL!

Break away from DEPRESSION!

ak away from DRUGS!

BOOK PURCHASE SPECIAL!

Thank you for your Purchase!

This COUPON entitles you to $2.00 off EACH AUDIO TAPE ORDERED!

(Mail order only)

REMEMBER!

INCLUDE THIS SPECIAL COUPON

WITH YOUR ORDER!

ORDER 24 HOURS A DAY!

7 DAYS A WEEK!

Visa or Mastercard Welcome!

38 WAYS TO REAFFIRM AND TAKE BACK YOUR LIFE!

BREAK AWAY SERIES

- 045 STRESS RELIEF & MANAGEMENT
- 046 SLEEP - DEEP & RESTFUL
- 047 OVERCOMING DEPRESSION
- 048 LEARNING THE ART OF RELAXATION
- 049 FREEDOM FROM ALCOHOL
- 051 EXERCISE MADE EASY
- 052 INCREASING YOUR ENERGY LEVEL
- 053 RELEASE YOURSELF FROMDRUGS
- 054 GUILT RELIEF - PEACE OF MIND
- 102 DEATH - COPING & UNDERSTANDING THE REALITY

SPORTS ACHIEVEMENT SERIES

- 083 GOLF - IMPROVE & WIN
- 084 TENNIS - IMPROVE & WIN
- 085 BOWLING - IMPROVE & WIN
- 086 RUNNING/BRISK WALKING - IMPROVE & WIN

HEALTH IMAGING SERIES

- 070 CANCER - STRENGTHENING THE IMMUNE SYSTEM
- 071 MS - IMPROVING MENTA L& PHYSICAL MOBILITIES
- 072 STROKE IMPROVING MENTAL & PHYSICAL RESPONSES
- 075 RELIEF FROM PAIN
- 076 GOOD HEALTH NOW (MIND, BODY & SPIRIT)
- 077 HEART (IMPROVING YOUR CARDIOVASCULAR SYSTEM)
- 078 HEADACHE RELIEF (CLEARMIND)
- 097 YES, I CAN FLY!

ACADEMIC ACHIEVEMENT SERIES

- 079 CONCENTRATION MADE EASY
- 080 ACCELERATED LEARNING & COMPREHENSION
- 081 BETTER STUDY HABITS
- 082 MEMORY IMPROVEMENT

SUCCESS NOW S

- 061 EFFECTIVE SPE (ONE-ON-ONE (GROUP)
- 062 TAKING CONTR YOUR LIFE
- 063 SUCCESS - UN YOUR CREATIV INNER-MIND
- 064 SALES, SUCCE PROSPERITY
- 065 ATTAINING WE POWER
- 067 SETTING & ATT REALISTIC GOA

SELF-IMPROVEMENT

- 055 STOP SMOKIN LIVING
- 056A WEIGHT LOSS (CHANGING EA HABITS)
- 056B WEIGHT LOSS ADVANCED
- 057 OVERCOMING PROCRASTINA
- 058 INCREASING SELF-CONFIDE SELF-ESTEEM
- 087 WEIGHT TRAIN CONDITIONING IMPROVE & W

AUDIO TAPE
ORDER FORM

$11.95
(each)

PLEASE PRINT

SHIP TO:

E:

ESS:

STATE, ZIP:

$11.95	4	47.80	8.00	39.80	← SAMPLE
PRICE	QTY	SUBTOTAL	COUPON DISCOUNT	AFTER DISC.	

SHIPPING & HANDLING

under $100.00 $4.95
over $100.00 $9.95

*All orders shipped UPS
Please allow 2-3 weeks for
delivery.*

SHIPPING &
HANDLING

6% SALES TAX
(MI RES.)

TOTAL

checks payable to:
**ieve Now Institute
23933 Eureka
aylor, MI 48180
(734) 287-2930**

CREDIT CARD INFORMATION

CREDIT CARD NUMBER

CREDIT CARD TYPE (VISA/MC)   EXPIRATION DATE

SIGNATURE

INVEST IN YOURSELF!

The best investment you could ever make!

SEMINARS AND SPEAKING ENGAGEMENTS

Norm Caldwell, Professional Speaker

Norm's high-spirited speaking ability has been demonstrated at various workshops, seminars and presentations
throughout the world.

Norm has improved the quality of life for thousands of people.
Working with major corporations, businesses, sales organizations, schools and health care organizations, helping clients reduce stress and feel better about life

Call now to check availability and to schedule dates for your event.

Achieve Now Institute
23933 Eureka
Taylor, MI 48180
Phone: (734) 287-2930

MY MOTHER'S
PUBLISHING HOUSE
23933 Eureka Road
Taylor, MI 48180
Phone: (734) 287-2930
FAX: (734) 287-7788

MY MOTHER'S PUBLISHING HOUSE

BOOK ORDER FORM

PLEASE PRINT

SHIP TO:

NAME: _____

ADDRESS: _____

CITY, STATE, ZIP: _____

PHONE: ( ) _____

CREDIT CARD INFORMATION

CREDIT CARD NUMBER

CREDIT CARD TYPE (VISA/MC)   EXPIRATION DATE

SIGNATURE

SHIPPING

- first book
.00 each
additional book
the U.S.A.

se allow 2-3
s for delivery.

Please send me _____ copies of
LUNCH BOX NOTES™
at $_____ a copy

Please send me _____ copies of
Here's A Thought!™
at $_____ a copy

SUBTOTAL	
6% SALES TAX (MI RES.)	
SHIPPING	
TOTAL	

MY MOTHER'S PUBLISHING HOUSE

23933 Eureka Road
Taylor, MI 48180
Phone: (734) 287-2930
FAX: (734) 287-7788

Make checks payable to:

1 - 5 BOOKS FOR $7.95 ea.
6 - 25 BOOKS FOR $7.45 ea.
26 - 50 BOOKS FOR $6.95 ea.
51 - 100 BOOKS FOR $6.45 ea.

(CALL DIRECT

Enjoy these Words of Wisdom
Here's a Thought!
These words have improved

PASS IT ALONG PASS IT ALONG PASS IT ALONG PASS IT ALONG

FEEL DOUBLE GOOD

LUNCH BOX NOTES

MY MOTHER'S PUBLISHING HOUSE

23933 Eureka Road
Taylor, MI 48180
Phone: (734) 287-2930
FAX: (734) 287-7788

THINK GOOD HEALTH
BEING DIFFERENT IS GOOD
Enjoy these Words of Wisdom
Here's a Thought!
These words have improved
LUNCH BOX NOTES

1 - 5		***BOOKS FOR $7.95 ea.***
6 - 25		***BOOKS FOR $7.45 ea.***
26 - 50		***BOOKS FOR $6.95 ea.***
51 - 100		***BOOKS FOR $6.45 ea.***

(CALL DIRECT for larger quantities)